THE FORMS
OF MUSIC

THE FORMS
OF MUSIC

André Hodeir

TRANSLATED FROM THE FRENCH
BY NOËL BURCH

WITH 16 ILLUSTRATIONS

WALKER AND COMPANY ❋ *New York*

Second Printing 1967

First published in France as *Les Formes de la Musique*, a title in the *Que sais-je?* series. © 1951, Presses Universitaires de France.

Copyright © this translation, including new material, 1966 by Walker and Company, a division of Publications Development Corporation.

Published simultaneously in Canada by George J. McLeod, Limited, Toronto.

Library of Congress Catalog Card Number:
65-15129

First published in the United States of America in 1966 by Walker and Company, a division of Publications Development Corporation.

Printed in the United States of America

PREFACE

Musicology has made tremendous strides in the past half-century; strides that affect not only the important areas of historical knowledge and research, but also the vital area of popularization. Certain deficiencies thus seem all the more surprising. One such is the absence of any comprehensive survey of musical forms. Anyone wanting information on a given musical form or theories about the evolution of that form must either be satisfied with a dictionary paragraph, necessarily incomplete, or spend hours poring over reference books of all sorts: histories of music, treatises on composition or aesthetics, monographs and so on.

This little book makes no pretense of even beginning to fill this gap. Its very length precludes any such ambition. Besides, I am neither a musicologist nor an aesthetician; merely a composer. And an artist may not be best equipped to deal with this vast, complex subject. Nor was it my intention to treat the problems of musical form and structure technically, which would have required long, drawn out analyses. My aim is to give the most precise possible definition of each musical form, a résumé of its history, and a brief study of its structures.

Presenting these different forms chronologically posed some insoluble problems; I therefore decided to follow an alphabetical arrangement; the student who has to get his information quickly will appreciate the advantage. This alphabetical arrangement is preceded by an introductory chapter designed to survey the problems to be touched on, and to establish a terminology. On this last point I have committed myself so deeply that I expect some sharp criticism. However, the terminology adopted in this book, even if guilty of going contrary to current usage, seems to offer certain advantages. Let the reader be the judge.

Although the number of musical quotations is deliberately small, the number of examples given is fairly large. As this is a popular book, I thought it best to refer the reader only to well-known works. Most of the titles mentioned figure frequently on radio and concert programs. On the other hand, it should come as no surprise that most of the examples are borrowed from the works of Johann Sebastian Bach. Inevitably a book dedicated to the discussion of musical forms must contain constant references to that master who provided the model for every form used in his day.

Finally, with each new edition I have had to alter certain definitions and qualify certain statements that no longer seem true, or that contradict the aesthetic positions I have progressively been led to take in the course of the many years separating the first edition of this little book from its present reissue. It might have been preferable to thoroughly recast the whole. Such as it is, I hope the reader will find it not completely riddled with imperfections.

A. H.

CONTENTS

Contents

Part One

GENRE, STYLE, FORM AND STRUCTURE

It may be useful to define at the outset certain terms that will appear frequently. This is not as simple as it may seem, especially if the reader remembers that even well-known aestheticians have argued about the exact meaning of such words as *form* and *structure*. I lay no claim to infallibility in matters probably outside my scope. Still, I shall try at least to be consistent: once I have defined my terms, I shall avoid presenting different, contradictory interpretations.

Four terms are in question: *genre, style, form* and *structure*. I shall propose definitions of these that will meet with the approval of musicians, if not of aestheticians.

GENRE.

There are two definitions of *genre*, which, though apparently quite different, are actually complementary. By the first, genre is a certain spirit that governs a work's conception; by the second, it is a family of forms having many common characteristics.

Distinctions between genres may be spiritual (sacred as against secular music) or technical (vocal as against instrumental music). More precisely, all overlap: sacred music—like secular—may be instrumental as well as vocal. Likewise vocal music includes both secular music (opera, secular cantata) and sacred music (church cantata, oratorio, Passion). These examples suffice to show the flexibility of *genre*. From subdivision to subdivision it even becomes difficult at times to determine exactly where the *genre* ends and

the *form* begins. The sonata, the trio and the quartet are obviously related forms that may reasonably be grouped in a
single family called chamber music. However, it is far more
difficult to associate, say, opera and operetta. Do these two
forms really fall under the single heading of lyric art? Is it
not obvious that their styles, even more than their structures,
conflict sharply? Is the sum of their resemblances in fact
equal to the sum of their differences? Would it not be more
reasonable to regard them as two distinct genres? No posi-
tive answer can be given to these last two questions.

Still, however vague and arbitrary, the concept of *genre* is
convenient and even necessary, for it allows us better to
delimit the problems posed by the concepts of *style* and
form.

STYLE.

The concept of *style* is more exact, yet no less complex.
We must examine it from two angles: in relation to the
composer, and as a function of the genre to which his composition belongs. Vis-à-vis the composer, we may call style a
kind of trademark the composer imprints on his idea, one
that, once realized through his technique, determines
whether the composition is original or not, depending on
whether he is gifted with a distinctive personality. Through
style a composition lives; style gives it characteristic features
and allows us to identify its author; absence of style makes
for a mediocre work. In this sense we may argue that style is
more important than form: Mozart's chamber music is obviously far more personal than—and stylistically far superior
to—that of his contemporaries despite its cleavage, by and
large, to the same standard mold: the "sonata form".

Style, in a more limited sense, can thus indicate the actual
signature of the composer. Just as in literature we refer to
Voltaire's or Albert Camus' way of writing as their style, so
we may speak of the style of Ravel. Here we allude not so

much to the creative ideas per se as to the methods used, the characteristic turn of this or that phrase. However, when a composer uses figures and methods specifically his own, we again deal with individual creative personality.

Style can also be viewed as a function of the genre or form to which the composition belongs. This association is by no means arbitrary. Moreover, it is frequently made: we have all heard or read such expressions as "in the style of the fugue" or "in the lyric style." Every genre, every form, best adapts itself to a style appropriate to it. The composer's problem is to find a "common ground" between his personal style and the genre in which he has chosen to work. This is an unconscious process when the composer is naturally inclined to express himself in a given idiom: Palestrina, even when using a secular theme, composed a mass more easily than a madrigal. Often such a "common ground" does not exist and the composer's efforts to find it lead to a discouraging compromise: Wagner abandoned chamber music; Schubert, despite all his efforts, never managed to write a good opera. Sometimes, however, the rejection of all compromise can rejuvenate a genre: e.g., Debussy's introduction of a new style into opera—but this is an exception to the rule.

Admittedly the relation of style to genre is infinitely more nebulous than that of style to personality. Thus there is practically no stylistic relationship between the *Barber of Seville* and *Pelléas*, which belong to the same genre, whereas it is impossible to deny the underlying affinity between *Pelléas* and Debussy's *Quartet in G minor*, compositions that, though belonging to genres diametrically opposed, were both written by the same composer. Later we will return to this problem of style and its relation to genre and form.

FORM AND STRUCTURE.

We all know what is meant by a *form:* a certain type of composition. The symphony is one form; the concerto an-

other. The symphony differs from the concerto in that in the
symphony the composer speaks a language exclusively orchestral, whereas the concerto involves the intervention of a
solo instrumental style that radically alters the composition's
essential nature.

The idea of form is infinitely harder to define. It seems
impossible to do so until we have covered in the most minute
detail all the related problems. First we must place this concept in its proper relation to the concepts of structure, genre
and style, and then evaluate the need for it.

Form generally denotes the way a composition is constructed. This definition is much too vague to be useful;
more, it adds to the confusion between *form* and *structure* (a
frequent confusion, as we saw at the beginning of this chapter). I prefer the definition proposed by Boris de Schloezer,
according to which *structure* is the articulation of various
parts with an eye to constructing a whole, whereas *form* is
that very whole, whatever it may be, considered as an entity.
We do not deal here, as the reader might think, with a single
concept considered alternatively from the synthetic and ana-
lytic viewpoints. The idea of form is infinitely broader than
that of structure. Undoubtedly the one includes the other:
some forms differ only in their architectonic details; but these
details alone rarely suffice to determine a form. If we compare
the structures of a Handel opera and a Debussy opera, they
seem to have practically nothing in common. The Handel is
cut up into neatly separated pieces: arias, recitatives, duets
and so on. The Debussy comprises a certain succession of
scenes in which the elements of the drama are organized
around a continuous melodic development, with an orchestral accompaniment that occasionally comments on the action through a *leitmotif*. On the other hand, a comparison
made from the viewpoint of form shows that the differences,
although more numerous than the similarities, are also less
basic, and that the primary goal of opera—the expression of

dramatic action through voices and instruments—is common to both.

It follows that the idea of form is bound up with deep-rooted aesthetic necessities, with the essential nature of the work, rather than with its structure. When a composer elects to write a string quartet, he does so mainly because he enjoys expressing himself in a four-part instrumental idiom. Structural problems come second. This is true even in an occasional work: when a patron commissions a trio or a mass, it is very rare for him to specify whether the trio should follow the sonata form, or the mass be written on a single theme. Certain isolated forms, conditioned by their very structures—the passacaglia, for example—evade this rule; and yet over the centuries composers have learned to call in question the tyranny of even the most rigid musical patterns.

We can also see that the idea of *form* may be associated with the notions of *genre* and *style*: with that of *genre* because it is obvious that certain forms belong to a particular genre—the sonata to chamber music, the mass to sacred music—and with that of *style* because, as we have seen, each genre best adapts itself to a style suitable to it. There is such a thing as a solo concerto style, insofar as this form is designed to set off an instrument against the orchestra; Ravel and Schumann alike, each in his own *personal* style, followed this *general* style. A Beethoven concerto differs from one of his sonatas, not so much in its structure (the structures are often nearly identical), as in its style: the composer's objective in a sonata was entirely different from that which he set himself in a concerto.

The problems raised by the *genre, form* and *style* of a composition are generally neglected, not only by the listener —who fails to realize that to understand a work (and therefore to derive joy and profit from it) he must be able to place it clearly—but also by the performer, who all too often devotes all his zeal to reproducing the written notes, that is to

say, the outer wrapper. But what is to be said of the problems of *structure*, which, nine times out of ten, remain a
closed book to listener and performer alike?

That the amateur should care less about the structure than
about the emotional content of a composition is, after all,
reasonable enough. Let us take a concrete example: a table.
To the extent that this table is not merely a household object
but a piece of artistic furniture, we may apply to it those
definitions of genre, form, style and structure previously dis-
cussed. For example, we may say that the table belongs to
the *genre* known as furniture, that it has the *form* of a dining
room table, and that it is in the Empire *style*. To define its
structure, we must specify how many pieces it is made of,
whether it has extension pieces, whether its legs are joined
by crossbars, and so on. Such details will obviously interest
the carpenter or cabinetmaker more than the ordinary con-
noisseur, for whom it may be enough to know that the table
is beautiful. Similarly the internal architecture of a sonata
movement may be a matter of indifference to the listener; the
professional, however, called on to perform it, should be
acquainted with every detail of its articulation.

By their very nature the problems of structure are technical ones, which can only be apprehended clearly by those
who have an adequate grounding in musical theory. We cannot ask an ordinary music-lover to be equipped to analyze
an organ chorale or a Bach fugue; that is the specialist's job.
Nevertheless no one can truly follow the various twists and
turns of a composition as it unfolds if he knows nothing of
its construction. This may be the basic reason for the indifference or hostility with which the majority of "first performances" are greeted; confused by unfamiliar themes whose
recurrence after a single exposition escapes them completely,
listeners often find themselves out of their depth from the
outset, even though the style of the composition may be more
familiar to them than its structure. The listeners have a confused impression of being lost in a sort of labyrinth of sound

and unable to find the exit. Since they lack the indispensable reference points, the most logically constructed musical discourse seems incoherent. It has often been observed that "the concert-going public likes only what it is well acquainted with." This would seem merely the direct result of that state of insecurity into which the public is thrown, in the face of every new work, by the lack of a guiding light in the form of an awareness of structure.

THE NEED FOR FORM AND STRUCTURE.

It may be premature to offer a precise definition of form. One major problem has not yet been examined: the profound need for form and structure. It seems possible to do this with some assurance of objectivity only by systematically casting doubt on the acquisitions of six centuries of Western tradition. The reader will understand that both the goal and scope of this book preclude such an attitude. We must confine ourselves to an empirical approach.

Is it absolutely necessary for a musical composition to have a form and a structure? Since music addresses itself more to the sensibility than to the intelligence, must the intelligence impose an organizational framework on what might otherwise be merely a series of sensations, pleasant or shattering, crude or refined? Is the art of sound more akin to architecture than to poetry? Should we not fear that an exclusive concern with rigorous construction may deprive musical expression of all spontaneity?

Such objections are by no means superfluous. There is no doubt about it: even perfect mastery of form will not suffice to create a valid piece of music; the example of certain polyphonists of the Middle Ages, for whom the elaboration of a canon in twelve or sixteen parts was an end in itself, is proof that a concern for form, when it serves as a substitute for emotion, can lead to mere formalism. However, although form is not an end in itself, it does not follow that it is useless. Even the labor of those polyphonists was not utterly useless: it prepared the ground for the wonderfully expressive, balanced art of the Renaissance. Besides, no great musical composition is completely devoid of form. Even the masterpieces of so-called impressionist music display, by their very "anti-formalism," a subtle concern with form that foreshadowed certain modern works whose structures have been described as "subterranean."*

The need for form becomes apparent as soon as we agree to regard musical discourse as an *instigator of situations*. Just as on the stage no line or gesture makes sense except in a previously established situation, so in music each recurrence of a theme, each succession of keys, each combination of motifs, can be clarified only by what has preceded.

Nor is it far-fetched to state that certain structural ideas, certain formal achievements, may be beautiful in themselves, and that the compositions resulting from them, though they may seem devoid of human emotion, may well be rich in aesthetic emotion. Does this "beauty of form," pure beauty if ever there was such, require that the listener be fully aware of the means through which it is embodied? Not necessarily. It is possible for the basic structures of a composition to remain unrecognized by the listener; it is possible for them to remain entirely "below the water line," so to speak, while

---

* Since, with very few exceptions, this book deals only with classical and pre-classical music, I prefer not to enter here into a discussion of the problems raised in recent years by the appearance of "aleatory" music and "controlled" as against "blind" chance. Such a discussion would lead us too far afield. Suffice it that although those composers who are enamoured of "mobiles" governed by "chance" ascribe a new meaning to the word *form*, a meaning many find disconcerting, they do not claim to be wholly unconcerned with form.

To a theologian the gods have nothing to with God; similarly the chief distinction between classical and contemporary music is the elimination of a plural that is only a hindrance for the composers of today: the musical forms are dead (they live on only in the masterpieces of the past), but form in music remains very much alive.

contributing effectively to the serene motion of the "ship." If we were to do away with certain imitations, certain underlying canons that the ear can barely detect and whose existence often comes to light only on analysis, many pieces by Bach would lose the essence of their innermost balance.

Art cannot coexist with chaos. Even jazz, that glorification of the senses, that music of a people for whom the physical joys are fundamental, is organized, obeys the principles of form and structure. The Western mind is satisfied only by that which approaches a certain sense of perfection inherent in it. It is this taste for perfection that compels the Western mind to shun mixed styles, and to strain toward perfectly balanced construction. Just as men, however different in constitution and behavior, are all born of a single cell, so a musical composition must develop from a single generating element. But unity is not synonymous with monotony. The secret of artistic creation lies in the artist's ability to extract, from this initial cell, a maximum of diversity; such is, for example, the technique of the *variation*, one of the purest forms of Western music.

It may appear that, so saying, we are rejecting bithematic and trithematic structures as impure; this, however, is not so. Even when they afford a contrast the two themes of a sonata are never heterogeneous. Each was conceived in relation to the other, and they cannot be considered separately. Indeed their very opposition gives rise to a kind of conflict, the result of which generally establishes the supremacy of one over the other; here, too, the principle of unity is maintained.

The tonal system, adhered to in Western music for more than three centuries, has been a tremendous factor in construction and unity. It provided the axis around which was organized the play of expositions, counter-expositions and developments that constituted the essential structural feature of the classical composition. But it is perhaps even more noteworthy that Arnold Schoenberg, who set out to liquidate the tonal system, organized the new atonal world on the basis of a technique, the twelve-tone row system, that insures, more rigidly than ever, the preeminence of the idea of Unity. Some may feel that there is nothing final about this organization; the fact remains, however, that Schoenberg's experiment confirms one of the permanent tendencies of Western music.

Leaving architectonics and returning to style, we find that the need for unity appears greater still. Certain forms with imperfect structures contain that minimum of balance which suffices to justify their existence. But we find no example of a *stylistically* heterogeneous work that retains any effectiveness. A mixture of styles is tantamount to an absence of style.

It is through the magic of style that the artist creates the universe in which his composition moves. If that universe is altered, there occurs a reversal of values that changes the color and meaning of those elements that seemed the most stable, rendering the composition unintelligible.

Thus the great concept of Unity, the ultimate focus of any discussion of form and structure—or of style—dominates the whole of Western art.

DEFINITION OF FORM.

We are ready now to define *form*. *Form is the means through which a composition strives to achieve unity.* The greater the diversity of means brought into play, the richer the form; the more the various elements introduced are coordinated into one homogeneous whole, the more nearly perfect is the form.

This definition has the advantage of bringing out the very essence of the composition. Indeed, what determines a given form? Here, it may be a certain type of theme (the chorale); there, an alternation, a dialogue (the concerto); elsewhere, a particular kind of writing (the organum). The permanence of that theme, that alternation between the soloist and the orchestra, that particular kind of writing, are *essential*; it is through them that the composition strives to achieve unity. To be sure, many forms (we might call them *architectonic forms*) are identified solely by their structures: the passacaglia derives its existence from its arrangement in sections, the rondo from its special pattern. Other more complex forms have several *raisons d'être*: the symphony can be explained by both its structure and its purely orchestral organization. Bringing the problem of form down to a simple question of structure is, as we have seen, a frequent error; but frequent as it is, it is nonetheless an error. We hope we have guarded against it here.

Part Two

THE PRINCIPAL
MUSICAL FORMS

AIR DE COUR

The French *air de cour*, whose historical career extends from the end of the sixteenth century to the middle of the seventeenth, is a minor vocal form. During its period the term covered all sorts of aristocratic or even popular love songs and pastorales, to the exclusion, however, of drinking songs, dance tunes and religious songs. Usually written for a single voice, the air de cour is less fully developed than the aria; the accompaniment was provided by a single lute, later replaced by the *basso continuo*.

Dramatic with Guédron, precious with Boesset, the air de cour constituted the principal element of the *ballet de cour*, which was very much in vogue during the reigns of Henry IV and Louis XIII. It died out by the end of the seventeenth century, supplanted on the cultural level by the arias of Lully and his followers, and on the popular level by the "vaudeville" or voice of the city (*voix de ville*).

STRUCTURE.

The air de cour is divided into "stanzas," and often comprises one or more *doubles* (see *Suite*), a kind of ornamental and improvised variation designed to show off the singer's virtuosity. The *ritornello* (flourish) and the *instrumental prelude* are optional.

ANTHEM

The *anthem* (from *anti-hymn* or *antienne*) is a specifically English form of vocal religious music; the *motet* and *cantata* are its Latin and German equivalents. Henry VIII gave the anthem its important place, when he imposed a new liturgy on his people at the end of the sixteenth century. The text was an English translation or paraphrase of passages from the Bible. Its dimensions were variable, since the form itself was not fixed but like the motet underwent various transformations from one century to the next. All the great English masters used it: Byrd and Gibbons in the polyphonic style, John Blow and especially Purcell and Handel in the monodic and concert style.

STRUCTURE.

At the end of the sixteenth century the structure of the *anthem* was similar to that of certain motets in polyphonic imitation. Later it came to resemble the cantata. Here we must distinguish between the *full anthem*, written for chorus, with or without instrumental accompaniment, and the monodic *verse anthem*, in which one, two or sometimes three soloists dominate. The *full anthem with verse* combines these principles.

ARIA

In a broad sense the *air* or *aria* is an extended vocal or instrumental melody, generally accompanied by the orchestra, and finds its place—perhaps its most important place—in every lyric composition: opera, cantata, oratorio and so on. In the instrumental suite the aria is a melodic section that, in contrast to the other movements, does not exhibit the character of dance music. The aria first appeared, like opera, at the end of the seventeenth century. Its evolution, in form as in style, is closely linked with that of opera as a whole.

STRUCTURE.

The aria can assume the most varied structures. In the seventeenth and eighteenth centuries it often embraced, even in opera, the two-part form that it takes in the instrumental suite, in imitation of the dance movements (Aria from the Suite in D, by J. S. Bach).

But the structure most current between the ends of the seventeenth and eighteenth centuries was the *aria da capo,* an important feature of Italian, and even French, opera (the analogy with the rondo is obvious). The aria da capo (*da capo,* "from the beginning") is summed up schematically by the figure ABA, which, as we shall see, is the most characteristic structure of Western music. After an instrumental ritornello the main part sets forth an extended period (A) based chiefly on the opening key. Then, in a related key (relative or dominant), a second period (B) supplies a di-

27

version. Finally, a ritornello is followed by a repetition of
period A. This form of aria is used in the same way by J. S.
Bach (arias from the *St. Matthew Passion*).

We also find, especially in Rameau, a type of aria in three
sections without repeats, which comes down to an ABC pattern. In this instance unity is slightly sacrificed to diversity,
but it is preserved on the level of tonal relationships: while
A, after establishing the main key, moves toward the dominant, and while B avoids the main key to end on the relative
(there are times when relative and dominant are reversed, A
moving toward the relative, B toward the dominant), the
third part of the piece always emphasizes the supremacy of
the initial key.

Certain seventeenth-century masters liked to construct
arias on a *ground bass* (q.v.). This pattern, like the one
above, was much less current than the aria da capo.

The *cavatina*, very popular in Mozart's time, is a rather
condensed form of the aria, in a single section; the repetitions of music or text, and the long vocal flourishes, typical
of the Italian aria styles, are generally omitted in the cavatina (Donna Elvira's Aria, *Don Giovanni*, Act I).

Finally, with Wagner, the aria ceased to be confined in a
rigid framework. Developing freely against an orchestral
background as important as the vocal part, it follows the text
so closely as to become identified with the *arioso* (*Tristan
and Isolde*).

ARIOSO

The *arioso*, essentially a vocal form, is a kind of *accompanied recitative* (see *Recitative*) with a very melodic, expressive character and a regular beat, to be sung "in the manner of an aria," as its name indicates, occupying a middle ground between the pure recitative and the aria. Examples occur as early as the beginning of the seventeenth century, in the first Venetian operas, especially those of Monteverdi. By the late seventeenth and early eighteenth centuries it had acquired considerable importance in certain types of opera or oratorio, preceding and introducing the principal arias (Handel, Bach). The subsequent evolution of dramatic style left little place for the traditional arioso, which fell into disuse. Nevertheless the spirit of the arioso continued occasionally to manifest itself. The Wagnerian melody, which has no definite structure and is sustained on a continuous symphonic foundation, is certainly much nearer to the arioso than to the recitative or the aria.

STRUCTURE.

Melodically the arioso is by nature fuller than the accompanied recitative; rhythmically it has more squareness and regularity: in this respect it resembles the aria, though it does not have the latter's proportions, or its construction in several parts. Still, certain composers—the most outstanding being J. S. Bach (the *St. Matthew Passion*)—subject it to a rigorous organization: the melody still develops freely, but within the framework of modulations imposed on it by the

29

orchestra. The task of the orchestra consists in developing a characteristic design, usually very brief. This use of a "modulating cell" gives Bach's arioso great unity, in no way impaired by the boldness with which the composer shifts from one key to another, which is sometimes very remote.

ART SONG

The definition of the *art song* corresponds to that of the *lied* (q.v.): it is a vocal setting, for one voice, of a short poem, usually accompanied by the piano. In practice the word *lied* is reserved for specifically German compositions, so that *art song* can be used to designate vocal chamber music that does not belong to any of the various Germanic schools.

The French *mélodie* has a number of features in common with the lied, especially its intimate lyric quality—as against the theatrical lyricism of opera—which is its essence. However, the two forms do differ in one respect, by no means negligible: whereas the German lied harks back to its folk origins (*Volkslied*), the French mélodie is resolutely aristocratic, refined and sophisticated. The term appeared in 1830 with Berlioz' *Mélodies Irlandaises*; but these pieces are hardly distinguishable from the *romance* (q.v.) then in vogue, except that they showed to some degree the influence of dramatic music; in fact Berlioz never wrote more than a few mélodies properly so-called. The mélodies of Gounod are also reminiscent of the romance; whereas Saint-Saëns and Lalo made a more marked departure from it, inspired as they were by the German lied. It was under this double influence that the French mélodie began to take shape; it did not, however, reach maturity until about 1875, with Fauré, Duparc, Chabrier and Chausson, of whom the first two at any rate are among the masters of the form. At the beginning of the twentieth century the mélodie found new life under Debussy, who gave us its masterpieces, in this form with his *Chansons de Bilitis*.

Outside France and the Germanic countries, the art song is dominated by the imposing figure of Mussorgsky, whose three cycles, *The Nursery*, *Sunless* and *Songs and Dances of Death*, composed between 1865 and 1875, were far in advance of what was then the French mélodie. They are known to have inspired Debussy.

STRUCTURE.

From the *romance* out of which it rose, the mélodie began by borrowing the strophic construction, whose weaknesses are well known: lack of flexibility, an inevitably distorted prosody from the second verse on, incompatibility of music and text, and lack of musical development. Duparc and Fauré, like Schubert before them, broke away from this overly rigid framework and introduced patterns based on the strophic form with variants, the da capo, and especially the technique of through-composition, already explored in the *lied* (q.v.). However, it was with Debussy that this last device acquired its full meaning. It was inevitable that impressionistic music, composed solely of suggestions and nuances, should reject all pre-established structures and follow only the words. For all that, however, Debussy was not entirely heedless of construction in his mélodies: witness the care with which he leads up to the re-entry of the opening pattern in *La Flute de Pan*.

BALLAD

The modern *ballad*, which first appeared toward
the end of the eighteenth century, began as a typical manifestation of German romanticism. Its only resemblance to
the medieval ballad (see *Medieval Forms*) was that it was
generally inspired by a literary text. Originally vocal, it follows the simple strophic structure of Goethe's ballads. It is a
composition to be sung with orchestral or piano accompaniment. A bit later it was expanded with the addition of
choruses (Schumann). Simultaneously it was extended into
the domain of instrumental music, without however, losing its
epic and narrative character, and so became a form of "program music," though less characteristic than the symphonic
poem.

BALLET

The *ballet* is a dramatic form in which the action
is expressed through pantomime and dance. It is generally a
composition for orchestra; at times, however, it may involve
singing. We distinguish between the ballet as an autonomous
form and the ballet inserted into an opera as a kind of
divertissement. One or the other has predominated by turn

through the history of the ballet, whose origins are in antiquity. In the fifteenth century the pure ballet was much in vogue in the French and Italian courts. The sixteenth century marked the appearance of the *masque* (q.v.), one of the most important forms of English dramatic music. Its French equivalent was the polyphonic *mascarade,* which in an expanded form became the *ballet de cour* (court ballet). The French court ballet, which was both instrumental and vocal, coincided closely with the first attempts by the Florentines to introduce dramatic monody (end of the sixteenth century). Up to the time of Lully it enjoyed a considerable vogue and was at the origin of a form invented by Molière and Lully, the *comédie-ballet,* a combination of spoken comedy, song and dance, and then of the *opéra-ballet,* a further development of the *comédie-ballet* on a lyric plane. In the seventeenth century the *opéra-ballet* was simultaneously in vogue in Germany and Italy under the name *balletto.* But it was in the seventeenth century that the French composer Rameau produced the masterpiece in this form with his *Indes Galantes.*

All these varieties of autonomous ballet were neglected during the classical and romantic periods, and ballet was not reborn until about the end of the nineteenth century. However, this rebirth became a dazzling resurrection in 1909, thanks to Diaghilev and his Ballets Russes. Diaghilev made the ballet the most meaningful of the dramatic musical forms of his day. The modern ballet aimed high: it aspired to complete dramatic expression solely through pantomime, dance and music. Whether or not it attained its goal, this concept gave birth to compositions of great breadth and lofty musical stature (Ravel's *Daphnis and Chloe* and Stravinsky's *Petruchka* and *The Rite of Spring*). As a parallel certain composers have tried to revive, in more modern form, the old *opéra-ballet* (Roussel's *Padmâvati*).

The interpolated ballet is also extremely old: in the fifteenth century the performance of tragedies included dances, with or without song, in imitation of the dancing choruses of the ancient theater. In the seventeenth century the Italian *intermezzo* (q.v.), the subject of which had nothing to do with the main action, was often a pretext for dances. In France the ballet, which was inserted into the opera to add zest to the performance, sought to bear some relationship to the action, even if it did not spring directly from it. This concept prevailed throughout the nineteenth century, when almost every Italian or French opera included at least one ballet. However, this type of decorative ballet has no place in modern musical drama, which is more concerned with psychological conflicts than with spectacular entertainment: in the works of Wagner, and in all the compositions that have grown from his dramatic concepts, the interpolated ballet has disappeared. This is one of the principal causes of the renaissance of the autonomous ballet.

STRUCTURE.

Like the opera, the ballet may be organized along two different patterns. The older of the two is simply a succession of set pieces, with each dance bearing a very individual stamp and clearly differentiated from the others. All interpolated ballets are related to this type. The modern ballet, on the contrary, is most often divided into "scenes," which follow one another almost without interruption.

CANTATA

The *cantata* is a relatively short lyric drama in several parts. Designed for the concert hall or the church service, it involves no dramatic action in the strict sense: one does not "act out" a cantata. It is necessary to differentiate the chamber (secular) cantata from the church cantata. Both belong to the domain of vocal music, although the role of the orchestra is by no means subsidiary. Like opera, the cantata appeared at the beginning of the seventeenth century, at the time of the introduction of accompanied monody.

The Florentines, Caccini and Peri, were the first to use this form, although they did not call it by its original name, the *cantada*. At first it was merely a short dramatic composition divided into fragments and sung by a single performer accompanied by a few instruments. With Rossi and Carissimi (middle of the seventeenth century), the cantata began to expand: the orchestra was developed, the number of characters increased and vocal ensembles made their appearance. In Bach's time relatively massive choruses were often introduced. From Italy the cantata passed into France, where Charpentier, followed by Clérambault, Rameau and Bernier, became masters of the secular cantata, while Du Mont and De Lalande, whose psalms and large-scale motets are very close to the church cantata, excelled in religious subjects. In Germany Keiser, Telemann and J. S. Bach cultivated both genres. Like many other forms born in the sixteenth and seventeenth centuries, the cantata, neglected by the classical and romantic composers, did not recover its

35

importance until the twentieth century, notably with Stravinsky (*Perséphone*). With his *Ode to Napoleon* Schoenberg proposed a new type of cantata for solo voice: the performer, accompanied by a chamber ensemble, declaims in accordance with the procedures of the *sprechgesang* (spoken melody). (See *Anthem, Concerto* (vocal), *Motet* (grand), *Oratorio* and *Villancico*.)

STRUCTURE.

In general, the traditional cantata is a composite form, combining several distinct forms into an organized unit. Originally these forms were the aria, the arioso and the recitative; then appeared the duet, more rarely the trio, finally the chorus, and in a number of German cantatas, the chorale. In the works of Bach, the undisputed master of the form, three principal types emerge: the cantata for solo voices, which includes only the recitative, the arioso, the aria, the duet and sometimes the trio (cantata No. 51); the chorale cantata, which is dominated by the vocal ensemble and is organized around a chorale (*Easter Cantata*); finally a third pattern achieves a "symbiosis" of the two preceding types (*Reformation Cantata*).

CANZONE

The Italian word *canzone* may be taken in its literal meaning of "song"; nevertheless we are concerned not with this essentially vocal form but with another form to which it gave birth: the instrumental canzone, or *canzone da sonar* (*sonare*, "to sound, or play, an instrument"). Originally (sixteenth-century Italy) it was a simple organ transcription of a vocal composition, and more particularly of French polyphonic songs. Later the Italian polyphonists (the Gabrielis in the sixteenth century, Frescobaldi in the seventeenth) composed original *canzoni*, but they were still concerned with adapting the vocal style to instruments (organ, brass or strings). The *canzone da sonar* is in part accountable for the development of the sonata.

STRUCTURE.

Like the closely related *ricercare*, the canzone comprises interlinking fuguelike episodes. However, in the canzone, the separate parts are more clearly differentiated: they are written alternately in three- and four-part time, with the fragments in three-part time constituting, as it were, variations on those in four-part time. (See V*ariation, Ricercare*.)

CASSATION

The *cassation* (from *cassazione*, "departure") is a kind of divertimento more particularly designed to be performed in the open air, and at night; hence its instrumentation, dominated by the wind instruments. Very fashionable during the period of the *fête galante* (second half of the eighteenth century), this form has fallen into complete disuse ever since. (See *Divertimento, Serenade*.)

CHACONNE

The *chaconne* is a very old dance of Spanish origin, in three-part time. Like the passacaglia, to which it is very similar, the chaconne made its appearance in the sixteenth century and acquired during the next century great importance as an instrumental form. It was sometimes incorporated into the suite, as a final section. The French composers of the seventeenth and eighteenth centuries associated it with the *rondo* (q.v.). At the end of the eighteenth century it was still frequently used in French opera as a ballet finale. The nineteenth century neglected this form, but there seems to be a tendency to revive it in the twentieth: drawing his inspiration from Bach's famous *Chaconne*, Bela Bartok placed one at the beginning of his *Sonata for Unaccompanied Violin*; Maurice Ravel's *Bolero* has been regarded as a specifically orchestral adaptation of the principle of the chaconne. (See *Ground, Passacaglia*.)

STRUCTURE.

Like the passacaglia and the ground, the chaconne consists of a series of expositions of the same theme; but in this form the generating design is not only varied in its accompaniment but may undergo changes that affect its basic outlines through a system of variations known as "thematic amplification." This is true of J. S. Bach's *Chaconne for Unaccompanied Violin*, in which the theme undergoes thirty-two melodic modifications that go far beyond simple ornamentation. (See *Variation*.)

38

Ravel's *Bolero* applies a new system of variations: the theme is presented in its entirety seventeen times, without alteration of either its outlines or accompaniment; the composer deliberately confines himself to transforming the orchestration.

CHORALE

The term *chorale* is given to a type of hymn that has been extremely widespread in Germany ever since the Reformation, and that is at the root of the entire Lutheran liturgy. It stemmed from the *Volkslied*, or German folk song, but the influence of certain popular non-Germanic forms and reminiscences of certain Gregorian chants may have played an important role in its creation. It first appeared at the beginning of the sixteenth century; Luther himself is thought to have written some. Treated in widely divergent manners by the German masters of the seventeenth century (Scheidt, Pachelbel, Boehm, Reinken, Buxtehude), the chorale inspired a whole school of polyphony that seems to have offered a refuge for the mystical spirit and musical concepts of the contrapuntists of the Middle Ages and the Renaissance. This art reached its zenith with J. S. Bach, whose approach to the chorale was extremely varied, embracing vocal, organ and even instrumental music. Like the fugue, the chorale fell somewhat into disuse from the middle of the eighteenth century on, although some musicians, like Franck and Honegger, have attempted, not unsuccessfully, to give it a new lease on life.

STRUCTURE.

We must distinguish the chorale from its polyphonic dressing. As we have seen, the chorale proper is merely a hymn. As such its structure has few complexities: it can be summed up as a division of the melody into more or less symmetrical periods, generally separated by *fermatas*, pauses. Often the two first periods are repeated (ABABCDEF). The first chorales, conceived to provide a new type of hymn for church congregations, were sung in unison. However, this kind of theme lends itself perfectly to the most sophisticated contrapuntal combinations, just as it adapts itself to a harmonic support. In this respect it differs from the *cantus firmus* of Gregorian origin; another difference, apparent by the seventeenth century, lies in its regular, four-square and rigorously tonal character. For while the early chorales, using only one- and two-beat values, seem far less complex than the Gregorian chant, even in its dessicated sixteenth-century form, each part displays a rhythmic independence well illustrated by the first phrases of the famous chorale known as "Luther's" (Fig. 1).

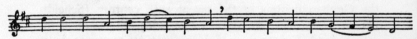

Fig. 1. "Luther's" Chorale. Original version. Opening.

If we compare the original version of this hymn with the version Bach wrote two hundred years later, it is easy to see that the chorale, during that period, lost in freedom and freshness what it gained in breadth and stability. This is because in the interim the bar line had appeared. And the musicians of the seventeenth century, in contriving to fit their melodies into the new system of musical metrics, often destroyed the rhythmic character that these melodies owed to the German language itself (Fig. 2).

Fig. 2. "Luther's" Chorale. Bach's version.

As for the structures that can be built from the chorale, we find at least a dozen different types in the works of Bach. Most derive from the variation. Among the patterns most frequently employed in his organ music by the master of Eisenach, the most important are:

1. The *contrapuntal chorale*, in which the chorale theme is usually presented in the upper part, while each of the other voices is heard in its own unbroken rhythmic and melodic design; sometimes a single rhythmic cell circulates from one intermediate part to another (the chorale *Nun komm der Heiden Heiland*, from the *Orgelbüchlein*).

2. The *fugal chorale*, which came from the vocal motet by way of the Italian ricercare: each phrase is followed by an episode that opens with a short fuguelike exposition (the chorale *Wir Glauben all'an einen Gott*).

3. The *figured chorale*, which differs from the foregoing in that the theme always enters in long values, preceded at the beginning of each episode by short-value entries in the other parts; this was a favorite device of the master organists of southern Germany in the seventeenth century (Pachelbel, Walther); J. S. Bach often used it, too, notably in his last composition (*Vor deinen Tron tret'ich*).

4. The *chorale in canon form*, in which the theme is accompanied by one or more canonic imitations, generally in octaves, in long values, or equal values, or else by diminution or augmentation (the chorale *In dulci Jubilo*, from the *Orgelbüchlein*).

5. The *ornamented chorale*, in which the theme is set forth in the upper part and embellished by numerous grace

notes and incidentals (the chorale O *Mensch, bewein' dein' Sünde gross,* from the *Orgelbüchlein*).

6. The *chorale with variations,* involving the successive use of all the different devices mentioned above, as well as all the others suggested by the technique of variation (Partita in G minor).

7. The *chorale fantasy,* which calls into play the same elements as the chorale with variations, but in a less rigorous, more composite manner (*Veni Creator*).

Besides these structures, peculiar to organ music, there are other types of chorale, more specifically vocal:

1. The *harmonized chorale,* generally written for four parts. The melody is in the upper part; the other parts, although treated contrapuntally, are almost always syllabic, meaning that each syllable is heard simultaneously in all the parts. This is the simplest type of chorale and also the one most frequently used in the cantatas and Passions (the chorale *Herzlich* from the *St. Matthew Passion*).

2. The *paraphrased chorale,* which combines a harmonized chorale, sung by the chorus, and a design in the form of a melodic variation played by a solo instrument from the orchestra (the chorale *Jesu, meine Freude*).

3. Sometimes the paraphrase is combined with a form more complex than the harmonized chorale: in the *St. Matthew Passion* the chorale No. 35 (*O Mensch, bewein'dein' sünde gross*) is treated as a partly fuguelike, partly figured chorale.

4. A still more complex construction is that of the first chorus in the same composition, in which the chorale theme is superimposed on a long vocal and orchestral fugue in double chorus.

5. The cantatas, however, contain other, simpler devices, such as the trio-chorale, also used in the organ music; here the melody is sung by the tenor, while the bass and the upper

part are generally entrusted to the instruments and weave the polyphony on a design borrowed from the first period of the theme (Trio section of cantata No. 140, *Wachet Auf!*).

Specifically symphonic uses of the chorale are less common (cf. Mendelssohn, Bruckner, Honegger, Berg).

CHORUS

The word *chorus* is commonly applied to every choral piece not related to a fixed form like the madrigal, the chorale or the polyphonic chanson. Although the chorus, as defined here, is rarely an autonomous composition, it is often encountered from the seventeenth century on in the cantata, oratorio and opera. Neither its structures nor its style is clearly defined. One of the masters of this form, Handel, liked to alternate the fugue style and the syllabic style of composition (*Hallelujah* chorus from *The Messiah*). The chorus is rarely written to be sung *a cappella*.

CONCERTO

We must distinguish several types of *concerto*: the vocal concerto, the concerto grosso and the concerto with soloist; the last two belong to the category of instrumental music.

THE VOCAL CONCERTO.

This is the *concerto da chiesa* (church concerto), which
first appeared at the end of the sixteenth century, with the
Gabrielis. It is a vocal composition of religious inspiration,
with instrumental accompaniment (sometimes confined to
the organ alone); in short, a kind of cantata (J. S. Bach gave
the name *concerti* to his cantatas). The term *concerto* comes
from the Italian word *concertare*, "to compete"; it refers to
the "competition" of voices and instruments. The vocal
chamber concerto made its bow in the first half of the seventeenth century, but at that time it was of little importance; it,
too, was bound up with the cantata.

THE CONCERTO GROSSO.

This, too, was as often a chamber concerto (*concerto da
camera*) as a church concerto; the character of the music
alone determined which. In this form the instruments "compete" with each other. The orchestra is divided into two
groups: on the one hand, the *concertino*, or soloists, and on
the other, the *ripieno* or *grosso*, that is to say, the whole orchestral mass, hence the name *concerto grosso*. It was first introduced in 1674 by a German composer named Schmelzer;
but it was the Italians, and especially Corelli, who organized
and developed the form. However, the most perfect models of
the concerto grosso are Bach's six *Brandenburg Concerti*.
The concerto grosso was finally abandoned in favor of the
sinfonia concertante (q.v.).

THE CONCERTO WITH SOLOIST.

This form first appeared at the beginning of the eighteenth
century, with Torelli. It differs from the concerto grosso in

that the group of soloists is replaced by a single instrument, which "competes" with the entire orchestra. Vivaldi and Handel developed this form. J. S. Bach wrote the first keyboard concerti. Then came the reign of the symphony, which caused a corresponding expansion of the concerto: the accompanying orchestra became larger, while the solo part made increasing concessions to virtuosity for its own sake, especially with the advent of Paganini and Liszt.

STRUCTURE.

The concerto lacks its own structure. Insofar as the vocal concerto was identical with the cantata, it followed the cantata's form. The plan of the concerto grosso follows that of the pre-classical sonata, bringing to it the added enrichment of a fuller instrumentation; thus the alternation of the *ripieno* and the *concertino*, by introducing an element of variety, made possible larger works. The same is true of the concerto with soloist, which was monothematic at first, then later adopted a second theme, like the symphony and the sonata. In the concerto the exposition is preceded by a kind of pre-exposition in which the principal themes are played by the orchestra before being stated by the solo instrument. Usually the development is only a pretext for the soloist's virtuosity, resulting in an alternation of "lyrical passages" and "brilliant" finger work that all too often makes this form seem terribly conventional.

The concerto normally comprises three movements. Each usually ends with a *cadenza*, a kind of brilliant peroration in which the soloist is no longer supported by the orchestra, followed by a repetition of the principal theme in the form of a coda. In the eighteenth century it was customary to improvise the cadenza; this, however, resulted in abusive virtuosity comparable to that which had already led composers to write their own *doubles* or *variations*. (See *Suite*.) Starting with

Beethoven, it became the custom to write out the cadenza in full. However, other masters had preceded him in this practice (J. S. Bach, in the Fifth Brandenburg Concerto).

DIVERTIMENTO

The *divertimento* or *divertissement* is a kind of instrumental suite, but in a freer form: the different pieces that it comprises (usually five or six, sometimes more) do not necessarily display structural affinities. Also, it is normally written for a group of solo instruments rather than a full orchestra.

It made its appearance about the middle of the eighteenth century, replacing the suite, of which it was an outgrowth. It differs from its contemporary, the classical sonata, in its simpler workmanship (little contrapuntal writing and very limited developments), its smaller dimensions (as against a larger number of movements) and its dancelike characteristics.

The divertimento was much in fashion in the second half of the eighteenth century: it was written for wind instruments, winds and strings, the pianoforte and so on. Ultimately it was absorbed by chamber music (quartets and quintets), only to reappear in the twentieth century (Stravinsky, Bartok) in a more condensed form and a less frivolous spirit.

ÉTUDE

The term *étude* should be taken in the sense of study, or research. However, in this case the object of study is twofold: on the one hand it concerns strictly musical values, and on the other it deals with instrumental technique per se. A well-conceived étude, then, should strike a fairly even balance between music and virtuosity; this is so with Chopin. The origin of the étude lies far in the past: practice pieces were being written for the organ in the fifteenth century, and for the harpsichord in the sixteenth. Bach's *Inventions* are actually a kind of étude. However, the term was used for the first time by Cramer and Clementi, toward the end of the eighteenth century.

The étude has no fixed structure. Its design is borrowed from various types: binary form, lied, or more rarely, rondo.

FANTASY

The fantasy is normally a piece of instrumental music of a "free structure," or, more exactly, one that borrows the structure, if not the spirit, of a related form: ricercare, prelude or sonata, according to the period. The fantasy originated in the sixteenth century. The seventeenth-century English virginalists adopted it under the name *fancy*, identifying it with the ricercare; the Italian and German polyphonists also used it. In the eighteenth century J. S. Bach treated the fantasy as a large-scale prelude (Fantasy and Fugue in G minor, for organ). It was completely transformed in the second half of the eighteenth century, becoming a kind of free sonata form (Mozart). In the nineteenth century the word generally came to mean merely an arrangement, a kind of potpourri based on the principal melodies of an opera (*Fantasy on Carmen*, by Bizet); such fantasies were very popular at the time, but aside from their extreme musical feebleness they no longer had anything to do with the original meaning of the term.

STRUCTURE.

The structure of the fantasy varies with the composers, and even with the individual compositions. In Froberger's work, for example, the fantasy displays a fairly rigorous construction resembling that of the canzone; it consists of a series of episodes treated in the spirit of the variation around a central theme. In Bach it may either be very structured (Fantasy in C minor for harpsichord) or very free (Fantasy in G major for organ). Mozart's famous Fantasy in C minor for piano is a long sonata allegro, whose tonal framework constituted a departure from traditional concepts.

FUGUE

The *fugue* (from the Italian *fugare*, "to flee") is a composition in contrapuntal style, based on the principle of imitation and the preponderance of a short but well-defined generative theme, called the *subject*. Appearing toward the end of the seventeenth century, it was bound up with the polyphonic tradition of the fifteenth and sixteenth centuries, of which it was in some ways the crowning achievement: in no other form is the relationship of the different parts so completely evident; no other form attains such perfect unity. Although in this respect it belongs to the posterity of the motet, the fugue seems most closely related to instrumental music. Still, it has often been successfully adapted to vocal forms: we need only mention the *Sanctus* from Bach's B minor Mass, the second part of which is a long six-part fugue.

In the fourteenth, fifteenth and sixteenth centuries the Italians gave the name *fuga* to ordinary canons. (See *Medieval Forms*.) Only after 1650 did the real fugue appear. It derived from the *ricercare* (q.v.), and differs from it in that it is organized to make better use of the possibilities of the tonal system and especially of key relationships. Moreover, while the ricercare, except for some rare exceptions, develops several themes in succession, the fugue normally draws its entire substance from one single subject. The evolution from ricercare to fugue was the result of a constant search for ever greater unity. Among the leading musicians who worked in this direction most important were the Gabrielis, Frescobaldi, Sweelinck, Scheidt and Froberger. By the end of the

seventeenth century the fugue, though a latecomer, was one
of the essential aspects of the idiom of the polyphonists of
both southern Germany (Pachelbel) and northern Germany
(Buxtehude). However, in the first half of the eighteenth
century, it was J. S. Bach who composed the most perfect
examples (*The Well-Tempered Clavichord, The Art of the
Fugue,* the organ *Fugues* and so on). Subsequently, although
the fugue style remained one of the bases of classical composition—*fugati* (fuguelike expositions) are plentiful in
classical and even romantic symphonies—less use was made
of it as a form in itself. However, Mozart, Brahms, Franck
and above all Beethoven gave new meaning to it, both technically and spiritually. In our times the fugue is too often a
mere academic exercise without real aesthetic significance,
although certain contemporary composers (notably Bela
Bartok in his *Music for Strings, Celesta and Percussion*)
have regarded it as more than that. The fugue is a tonal form
par excellence, and does not yet seem to have been successfully integrated into the contemporary world of sound, which
tends more and more to reject tonality.

STRUCTURE.

We must differentiate between the *scholastic fugue,* a kind
of archetype, and the fugue per se, or *free fugue.* The scholastic fugue has only academic value: infinitely more conventional than the free fugue, it lends itself better to analysis.
For this reason we shall use it for illustration.

The *scholastic fugue,* written for four "voices," comprises
an *exposition,* a *development* and a *stretto.* The exposition
includes: (1) the statement of the *subject;* (2) the entry, in
another voice, of the *answer;* (3) the *subject* again, entering
this time in a third voice; (4) the entry of the *answer* in the
fourth voice.

The *answer* is simply the *subject* transposed into the
dominant key; this transposition, by altering the interval

relationship—the dominant-tonic (a fourth) is smaller than the tonic-dominant (a fifth)—makes necessary certain melodic modifications; however, these are not important enough to alter the theme's profile.

Starting from the second entry, the subject and answer are accompanied by a contrapuntal design, called the *counter-subject*, which, when it shifts from the dominant to the tonic key, undergoes the same modifications as the subject itself.

If the *subject* is very short, the four entries may not be enough to constitute a well-balanced exposition; in that case the next step is a *counter-exposition* composed of four new entries (sometimes only two), starting this time with the answer.

The development. While the exposition establishes the main key and its dominant, the development involves a series of modulations, making it possible for the subject, always accompanied by its counter-subject, to be heard in each of the four most closely related keys. Each entry of the subject is separated from the next by short *episodes* in imitative style, the elements of which are usually borrowed from the subject or the counter-subject. In general, the development ends in a dominant pedal point, thus preparing for the return of the original key.

The *stretto* may be regarded as the peroration of the fugue. It comprises a series of canonical entries of the subject and real answer, in increasingly close succession (*stretto* means "close, narrow"). All these canons or *strette* are usually truncated to some extent, except for one, called *stretto maestrale*, consisting of the complete subject and its answer in the original key.

The *free fugue* written for two, three, four, five or even more voices obeys no precise rules. Its elements are the same as those of the scholastic fugue, but they are combined much less rigidly, much less predeterminedly. J. S. Bach liked to construct each fugue differently, in dimensions that

ranged from the short fugue for harpsichord to the monu-
mental organ fugue, and his works provide an unequaled
wealth of examples.

Among his most famous fugues the sixteenth fugue in the
first book of the *Well-Tempered Clavichord* is often cited as
coming closest to the scholastic fugue (Fig. 3). It is written

Fig. 3. *The Well-Tempered Clavichord* (J. S. Bach), I, XVI. S, subject; R, answer; CS, counter-subject.

for four voices, in G minor. The subject, quite short but
sharply defined, enters in the "alto" voice, the answer in the
"soprano"; the modification here concerns the interval between the two first notes of the answer. Parallel to the answer the "alto" introduces the counter-subject, which, being
capable of inversion will be frequently found above the subject or answer in the course of the fugue. The third entry—
the subject in the "bass," accompanied by its counter-subject
in the "soprano"—is separated from the second by a one-
measure episode, a device employed fairly often to fill out
the exposition when the subject is brief. The entry of the
answer in the "tenor" (with the counter-subject in the
"bass") ends the exposition, which covers seven measures.
The development that follows comprises twenty measures. It
opens with a four-measure episode built on the tail of the
subject. This episode is static at first, then finally moves
toward the key of B flat, which is related to the principal
key. The entry of the subject in this new key takes place in
the "alto" voice (with the counter-subject in the "tenor");
then the answer in the relative dominant is provided by the
"bass" (with the counter-subject again in the "tenor"); the

composer takes advantage of this modulation to let the subject be heard in the soprano in the key of F major (counter-subject in the bass). The second episode consists of a series of modulations, three and a half measures long, from F major to C minor, which is the subdominant. It is composed of a canon at the fifth of the subject, which opens in B flat and then, toward the end, shifts unexpectedly to E flat major; the transition from this key to C minor is achieved after a brief incursion into F minor, by means of some three-part imitations by contrary motion on the tail of the subject. Similarly the transition into the subdominant and the third episode are both written for three parts. The entry of the subject in the subdominant takes place in the bass (with the counter-subject in the alto), then in the soprano (with the counter-subject in the bass). The composer is careful to present the answer in the dominant of the subdominant, in other words, the original key; but precisely because it is based on the answer this phrase in no way resembles a re-entry of the theme in the main key; moreover the answer (in the "alto") and the counter-subject (in the "soprano") appear here in a slightly ornamented form. It is the task of the third episode to lead the fugue firmly back to the main key: it achieves this in the space of three and a half measures by a series of rapid modulations to the most closely related keys, utilizing the tail of the subject as its chief motive throughout. A seven-measure finale provides the composition with a brief but entirely adequate conclusion, considering the shortness of the piece as a whole. The composer could have gone on developing this last part, instead of being content with this hint of a double stretto, consisting of two elements taken from the subject—the head and the tail—combined with the counter-subject. He preferred conciseness to fullness; his choice of a subject had already inclined him in that direction.

We have analyzed this fugue because it is one of the shortest and least complex of all those written by J. S. Bach.

Obviously Bach's fugues constitute a whole universe, which cannot be condensed into a single example, however well-balanced; we would have to examine the entire output of the master of Eisenach. We shall merely cite a few of the most significant pieces, taken from the first book of the *Well-Tempered Clavichord:* fugue No. 4, with its two subjects; fugue No. 20, the most highly developed in the book, in which the constant presence of the theme, alternately stated forward and backward, suggests some gigantic stretto; fugue No. 8, an amazing collection of contrapuntal combinations and imitations; and so on.

GROUND

The *ground* or *basso ostinato* is both a technical device and a form (in this case, the device fostered the form). It first appeared in sixteenth-century England, Spain and Italy, although we cannot say for sure which country was its birthplace. The ground was in vogue in all the instrumental music of the seventeenth century: the English virginalists as well as the harpsichord composers of the Latin countries made abundant use of it, after which it passed into vocal music as well (Monteverdi, Purcell). Forsaken throughout the classical period and the nineteenth century, the technique of the ground, if not the form, has reappeared in certain modern compositions (Jolivet's *Quartet*). (See *Passacaglia* and *Chaconne*.)

STRUCTURE.

The principle of the ground is that of a continuous bass supporting the melodic development and determining the harmony of the composition; the same pattern (*ostinato*) is repeated over and over, while the other parts construct a different verse on it each time; the analogy with such similar forms as the *chaconne*, the *variation* and especially the *passacaglia* is obvious.

The ground can be combined with other forms, some of which seem far removed from it. Such is the case with the main aria from Purcell's *Dido and Aeneas*, a perfect example of what might be called "controlled melodic invention." At first this famous air does not seem the result of any specific technique. Nevertheless it is rigorously built on a *basso ostinato*. Each of the four phrases of which it is composed is subtended by the same bass figure (Fig. 4). From their perfect juncture the song's melodic continuity is born. However, the composer was able to avoid the structural rigidity that would have resulted from an excessive symmetry of melody and bass; thus A′, the continuation of A, is considerably shorter: by ending as it does on a semi-cadence it supplies a respite essential to the economy of the composition; further on, the way B overlaps on both sides of the bass design also destroys the symmetry of the periods, while B′, which is shorter, re-establishes the sense of balance.

Fig. 4. *Dido and Aeneas* (Purcell). Dido's aria. The four phrases A, A', B and B' all overlap against the same bass pattern.

IMPROMPTU

The *impromptu* is a short instrumental piece, semi-improvisational. Its structure is not fixed, but follows usually the ABA pattern. It was very popular among the keyboard composers of the nineteenth century, especially Schubert, Chopin and Fauré.

INTERMEZZO

The *intermezzo* is a minor form of musical drama that had a certain historical importance. It originated in the fifteenth-century *entremets* (literally, "side dishes") and blossomed toward the end of the next century. Marenzio and Cavaliero are often cited, along with other composers of the period, for the intermezzi they composed for the wedding of Ferdinando de Medici, held in Florence in 1588. At that time the intermezzo was a musical entertainment inserted between two acts of a tragedy. It was predominantly in the madrigal style. The new Florentine style came in about 1600, and the intermezzo became a kind of minature opera, with singing and dancing. Subsequently it became the custom to insert intermezzi into the Italian *opera seria*. These had nothing to do with the main action. On the contrary, the intermezzo was soon organized so as to foster a different, generally comic parallel action, which even contained a hint of parody. This was the origin of the *opera buffa*: Pergolese's *La Serva Padrona* is midway between these two forms.

The intermezzo, which existed only in Italy, disappeared during the eighteenth century, supplanted as a genre by the *opera buffa*, and replaced in its function by the *ballet-divertissement*. (See *opera buffa*, under *Opera*.)

INVENTION

The *invention* is a brief instrumental piece, a very concise kind of étude, constructed by very strict rules. At least this is the form it takes with J. S. Bach, one of the very few masters to have treated this form. His two- and three-part *Inventions* bring to bear a polyphonic idiom in which the techniques of invertible counterpoint and canon predominate. In the twentieth century Berg further developed this form, introducing a series of inventions into his opera *Wozzeck*.

LIED

The *lied* is a vocal setting of a short poem for solo voice, usually with piano accompaniment. It is customary to distinguish it from the French mélodie and the art songs of other traditions (particularly the Russian tradition, of which Mussorgsky is the master), despite the fact that, formally, they are almost, but not quite, identical. (See *Art Song*.)

Within the German tradition we must also distinguish between the *Volkslied* (folk song) and the *Kunstlied* (art song). The first originated in the Middle Ages; it is older than the chorale, to which it gave rise. The second, the *Kunstlied*, with which we are here particularly concerned, appeared about the middle of the seventeenth century; Heinrich Albert is said to have been responsible for its codification, if not its invention. The first *Kunstlieder* derived partly from the German *Volkslied* and partly from the Italian aria. But it was not until the late eighteenth century that the great German composers took an interest in this form. Even so, Gluck, Haydn and Mozart paid it scant attention. It was Beethoven who ushered in the romantic lied, which promptly reached its zenith with Schubert and was handled with equal felicity in a different style by Schumann. Both borrowed their texts from the greatest poets of their day—Goethe, Schiller and Heine—achieving a rare blend of the most inspired poetry and the most poignant music. Brahms was the last representative of the golden age of romantic lieds. However, Hugo Wolf and Mahler, and later Schoenberg, Berg and Webern, tried to rejuvenate the form. With Mahler the

orchestra began to replace the piano accompaniment;
Schoenberg steered the lied toward chamber music and
dramatic music: *Pierrot Lunaire*, with its *sprechgesang*
(spoken melody) and its small instrumental ensemble, is
midway between the lied and the cantata.

STRUCTURE.

The *Kunstlied*, or German art song, usually borrows the
stanza construction of the *Volkslied*, in which the text alone
changes with each stanza, the music remaining unchanged.
Schubert often followed this simple type of construction:
many of his *Lieder* are strictly strophic (divided into
stanzas). The strophic structure may include, as concerns
the text, verses and refrains (*Ungeduld*); however, the refrain is not indispensable; in both cases, the music remains
unchanged. More often, Schubert introduced modifications
of detail, sometimes fairly important ones, into the melodic
line or the accompaniment of a verse whenever he was
tempted to by the text. This was the origin of the strophic
construction with variants (*Gute Nacht*). A third structure
is known as through-composition; here the composer allows
himself every liberty in order to follow the flow of the poem
(*Der Erlkönig*). Sometimes he even resorts to recitative
(*Der Doppelgänger*). Finally, a fourth type of structure is
based on the repetition of the opening period, following an
interpolated central episode, usually more violent, which
offers a contrast with that period (*Ihr Bild*); this ABA pattern is none other than that of the Italian aria, whose influence in the Germanic countries in the seventeenth and eighteenth centuries is well known. Moreover it is curious to note
that this ABA arrangement is basically what we call the *lied
form* in instrumental music.

The piano part, which blossomed and acquired expressive
importance at the beginning of the nineteenth century, finds
the most favorable terrain for its expansion in lieder cycles.

Schumann's preludes and especially his postludes are more
than simple transitions designed to join one lied to another:
they are often as long as the vocal part and may be regarded
as authentic musical commentaries. These sets of songs contain only hints of cyclical construction: Beethoven in *An die
Ferne Geliebte*, and Schumann in *Freuenliebe und Leben*,
did no more than introduce a few elements from the first lied
into the last.

THE LIED FORM.

The structure known as "lied form" belongs primarily to
the domain of instrumental music. It particularly concerns
the slow movements of the classical sonata, concerto and
symphony. It doubtless derives its name from the singing
character this movement assumes, in contrast with those
around it: the structural analogy of pattern that may sometimes be observed between, say, a Beethoven adagio and the
vocal *Lieder* of Schubert and Schumann is entirely superficial.

The lied form is a three-part construction somewhat reminiscent of the aria da capo. The characteristic feature of this
structure is that each of the three sections of which it is
composed is subdivided in turn into three episodes, according to a pattern that may be expressed as follows:

I. (A); a: opening design, which moves toward the
dominant.

   b: modulating episode, also ending on the
   dominant.

   a': re-exposition of a, but ending on the tonic.

II. (B); central modulating section, divided in the same
way: aba'.

III. (A); repeat of I, with slight variations in the writing.

This layout was much in use in the time of Haydn and Mozart (Adagio from the D major Piano Sonata, K. 576). Beethoven added a number of variants, such as the *developed lied*, which includes a second modulating central passage (ABA' CA"); the *lied-sonata*, a kind of sonata form without the middle development in which the theme A is divided into three parts; and the *lied with variations*, in which each new exposition of the lied theme (A) is followed by a variation.

LIGHT OPERA

Light opera, or as it is known in France, *opéra-comique*, was originally distinguished from grand opera by its subject matter and its style, the lightness of which justified a far more extensive use of the spoken word. However, toward the end of the nineteenth century, *opéra-comique* broadened its scope, treating subjects that had hitherto been reserved for grand opera, and very similarly. It has therefore become difficult to give a precise definition of this "form."

Opera buffa, the Italian equivalent of *opéra-comique*, was the offspring of the *intermezzo* (q.v.), which traditionally filled in the intermissions in *opera seria*. It first began to develop at the start of the eighteenth century, with Logroscino and Pergolese. At first it was simply a farcical parody of *opera seria*, but soon the form found an organization and style of its own, and comedy plots replaced the ancient Greek and Roman subjects of *opera seria*; as a result dramatic construction freed itself to some extent from the trammels of convention and became infinitely more lively.

Not only did *opera buffa* give the operatic genre a "shot in
the arm" particularly pleasing to the public of that period,
but also it offered certain aesthetic advantages that soon
became apparent: during the second half of the eighteenth
century most of the important lyrical compositions belonged
to the new form. Moreover Pergolese's *La Serva Padrona*,
performed in Paris in 1752, touched off the famous "Battle
of the Buffoons," which gave birth to *opéra-comique*
through the works of Rousseau, Philidor, Monsigny and Gré-
try. At almost the same time Hiller, in Germany, set himself
up as the initiator of a specifically German form of light
opera based on the lied, to which he gave the name *singspiel*.
However, it was Mozart, inspired by the Italian school of
Cimarosa and Paisiello, who provided the masterpieces of
German light opera, foreshadowing the coming expansion of
the form, which reached its culmination a century later in
Georges Bizet's *Carmen* (a development that, by reaction,
brought about the rise of operetta). Meanwhile the nineteenth century had confirmed the decline of the Italian *opera
buffa*, whose last major manifestation was Rossini's *Barber
of Seville*, and the rise of the French school. Today, despite
a few interesting attempts, light opera seems to be having as
hard a time renewing itself as grand opera.

Opéra-comique and *opera buffa* borrow their structures
directly from the old-fashioned opera in set pieces. However,
the recitatives sung in *opera seria* are often replaced in light
opera by spoken dialogues, as in the original version of
Carmen.

MADRIGAL

The *madrigal* is a vocal piece of extremely free style and structure. Very different from the Florentine madrigal (see *Medieval Forms*) of the fourteenth century, which was written for a single voice with instrumental accompaniment, the sixteenth-century Italian madrigal with which we are here particularly concerned is in polyphonic style. It was usually for five parts, *a cappella* until it became an accepted practice to replace the voices with instruments. It was born of the fusion of two styles: the Italian *frottola* and the Franco-Flemish *polyphonic chanson*. Besides which, the first madrigalists were not Italians: Arcadelt, Willaert, Verdelot, Cyprien de Rore. A second generation, more specifically Italian (Claudio Merulo, Ingegneri, Ph. de Monte, Nanini, Palestrina), started the movement that was to lead the madrigal to its highest point. However, not until the last quarter of the century did the masters of the third generation—Marenzio, the Gabrielis and especially Gesualdo and Monteverdi—perfect the more varied style of the chromatic or expressive madrigal, with its bold harmonic idiom. Subsequently, under the impetus of Monteverdi, the madrigal began a development made inevitable by the aesthetics of the period: the polyphonic style was supplanted by monody and the *basso continuo*; duets, trios and recitatives made their appearance, producing the *accompanied madrigal*, which was soon to become the *dramatic madrigal* (seventeenth century), a form much nearer to the cantata than to the madrigal *a cappella*. The *a cappella* madrigal, however, had a fertile posterity in other countries: not only did Roland de

64

Lassus, Claude le Jeune, Hassler, Sweelinck and many other Continental masters adopt it, but a whole school of madrigalists appeared in England at the end of the sixteenth century. Composers like Byrd, Morley, Gibbons, Weelkes, Dowland and Willbye produced a series of compositions slightly different in style but closely related in spirit, and all every bit as admirable as those of the Italian polyphonists.

STRUCTURE.

The structure of the madrigal is all the more difficult to define as it has so many different facets. We shall confine ourselves to the two principal forms, the *expressive madrigal* and the *dramatic madrigal*. The first differs from the French polyphonic chanson by its greater suppleness: it is more rigidly subject to descriptive considerations, and the alternation of polyphonic episodes with episodes written in a syllabic style often seems quite whimsical. In the second type the introduction of the recitative style and of duets, trios and choruses alternating with monodic passages suffices to show the close kinship between this form and the then embryonic cantata: although Monteverdi's *Combatimento di Tancrede e Clorinda* is called a madrigal, it is actually a cantata.

MASQUE

The *masque*, a typical form of sixteenth- and seventeenth-century English dramatic music, bears a certain relation to the *mascarade* and to the French *ballet de cour*.

(See *Ballet*.) It was a kind of entertainment involving allegorical, mythological and satirical scenes. It incorporated singing and dancing with an instrumental accompaniment. Like the French mascarade, the sixteenth-century masque was polyphonic in style; the choruses were written in the spirit of the madrigal. In the seventeenth century the monodic style became predominant. This form, employed by the leading English composers of the period (Gibbons, Purcell), gave impetus to the efforts carried out in the second half of the seventeenth century to create a specifically English opera. But neither the masque nor the embryonic English opera survived beyond the eighteenth century: the overwhelming success of Italian opera with the British public explains this twofold disappearance.

MASS

The *mass* is probably the most important, if not the oldest, form of sacred music. It is a composite vocal form, comprising five distinct parts, corresponding to the five prayers sung in the *Ordinary* of the Roman Catholic mass. Its origins are in the dawn of Christianity, certainly no later than the highest Middle Ages.

From the era of the Gregorian chant seventeen masses have been preserved, composed between the tenth and the fourteenth centuries. The first polyphonists (twelfth century) set a few *Kyries* or *Glorias* to music, but not until the fourteenth century did there appear the first four-part masses, in which the different prayers are treated in a similar spirit (*La Messe Nostre Dame,* by Guillaume de Machaut, mid-fourteenth century). With Guillaume Dufay (fifteenth century) the generative theme was introduced, in the form of a fragment of a Gregorian or secular melody, insuring the work's formal unity; at the same time the rapid development of the polyphonic style resulted in the sixteenth-century masterpieces in this genre, by Josquin des Prés, Palestrina and others.

Although the polyphonic masses of the fifteenth and sixteenth centuries were conceived to be performed *a cappella,* instruments were sometimes called in to reinforce sections inadequately filled out. In the same way, under the influence of the Florentine madrigalists and their Ars Nova, the traditional Gregorian melody, the only one in use to the fourteenth century, gradually gave way to secular melodies. Toward the middle of the sixteenth century, however, a vigorous reaction set in against the contemporary masters' abusive use of folk themes and contrapuntal artifices that made the text unintelligible, and against the use of instruments. The Council of Trent introduced a new aesthetic into sacred music. Palestrina was instructed to carry out the ecclesiastical directives, but nonetheless composed several masses based on secular themes.

The mass is one of the rare forms that remained strictly polyphonic through the seventeenth century: Monteverdi's masses were uninfluenced by the close proximity of the composer's operas or by the emergence of the new opera form in his own work: they might have been written by Palestrina or Victoria. Not until the end of the century did the Venetians (Caldara, Lotti), breaking with tradition, introduce the orchestra into the mass, treating each verse of the *Kyrie* and the *Gloria* separately in the form of an aria, duet or chorus—in short, turning the concert mass into a kind of cantata—a concept taken up again and even further devel-

oped by Bach in his gigantic B minor Mass (1733–1738).
Then, with Haydn, Mozart and Beethoven, symphonic and
operatic styles were "injected" in the mass; they remained an
integral part of it throughout the nineteenth century, during
which time the mass was regarded more as a composition for
concert performance than as church music, especially since
the great romantic composers turned their backs on the
Ordinary mass in favor of the *Requiem* mass (see *Requiem*)
and its more dramatic text.

Finally, several attempts have been made in the twentieth
century to restore the liturgical character of this form
(*Masses* by Caplet, Jolivet, Stravinsky). However, the
steady musical decline of the mass, from the sixteenth century right up to our own times (with the glorious exceptions
of the B minor Mass and Beethoven's *Missa Solemnis*)
seems indeed related to the general decline of religious
feeling.

STRUCTURES.

The *Ordinary* of the Roman Catholic mass involves five
principal cantos: the *Kyrie*, the *Gloria*, the *Credo*, the
Sanctus (together with its *Benedictus*) and the *Agnus Dei*.
According to the period and its tendencies, the musical set-
tings of these five unvarying texts produced very diverse
structures. Here we shall cite three:

1. *Gregorian mass.* This is written for one part *a cappella*.
The unity of the five sections of the mass is insured solely
through the use of a single mode. (See *Medieval Forms.*)

2. *Polyphonic mass.* The sixteenth-century mass, together
with the motet, is the highest expression of sacred polyphonic
music. Its structure is apparently as simple as its writing,
based entirely on contrapuntal imitation, is complex. A single
theme, nearly always borrowed from the Gregorian repertoire,

from a polyphonic motet, or from a secular chanson* provides material for the entire composition. The plan of the
work is determined by the text. Thus, for example, the *Kyrie*
is divided into three phrases: *Kyrie, Christe, Kyrie*, each of
which corresponds to a melodic design drawn from the
theme. Each episode gives rise to a kind of fugal exposition,
with each part entering successively in mutual imitation of
the others. Here and there the phases are linked by over-
lapping: the final cadence of each phrase already contains
the leading motif of the next. The greater length of the
Gloria and the *Credo* allows, at times, greater freedom.
Many masses are "parodies": all their elements come from a
previous motet by the same composer. There is not a single
theme in Palestrina's mass *Assumpta est* that does not derive
more or less directly from some component of the motet of
the same name. (See *Motet*.)

Another and older type, but one that Palestrina often employed, is the mass based on the *cantus firmus*, a motif
borrowed from the plain chant, which shifts from one part to
the other or is repeated in the same part, in long values, in
the style of a chorale theme (Palestrina's mass, V*eni Creator*); in any case this type of mass was undoubtedly the
origin of certain forms of chorale, and by the same token,
certain forms of variation.

3. *Concert mass*. This type mass is unquestionably related to the cantata, even though the recitative and the
chorale are absent. It contains arias, duets and choruses.
When the composition is vast, the traditional division into
five or six sections is abandoned in favor of a smaller frag-
mentation that converts each verse into a separate piece,
which often assumes a form different from that of the other
verses of the same prayer. Thus Bach's *B minor Mass* comprises no fewer than twenty-four numbers: fifteen choruses,
six arias and three duets, all with orchestral accompaniment

* This explains the titles of certain masses: Palestrina's mass, *Assumpta est*; R. de Lassus' mass, *Douce Mémoire*.

(although certain choruses are more archaic in style, written as they are in the spirit of *a cappella* polyphony, with the instruments simply doubling the voices).

MEDIEVAL FORMS*

Under this heading we have grouped all the principal forms that gave impetus to the music of the Middle Ages. Certain forms, like the polyphonic mass and the motet, will only be mentioned here, since their later developments are so much more important that it would be a mistake to treat them within the necessarily restricted framework of "medieval music"—unless we are to accept the thesis, admittedly quite defensible, that holds that musically the Middle Ages extend to the end of the sixteenth century. Other forms, on the contrary, scarcely survived past the middle of the fifteenth century, generally regarded as the end of the Middle Ages; it is these we shall discuss in this section. Considered in this light, the Middle Ages were a huge testing ground from which the splendid Franco-Flemish, Italian, Spanish and English schools of the sixteenth century all profited. The fact that the Middle Ages were primarily a laboratory period for the development of the polyphonic idiom in no way detracts from the perfection of certain medieval compositions and only serves to underscore the genius of their creators: Léonin, Perotin, Adam de la Halle, Machaut, Landini, Dunstable, Binchois, Dufay.

---

* This section, for clarity, is arranged chronologically rather than alphabetically.

GREGORIAN FORMS.

The Gregorian plain chant, codified at the end of the sixth century by Pope Gregory I, who gave it his name, was both the result of a thousand years of monodic (unison) singing and the foundation on which the art of polyphony was to be built several centuries later. Essentially liturgical, it had its roots in the Hebraic psalms, and grew gradually richer through contributions from the various sources of pagan tradition: Syria, Egypt, Rome and Greece. St. Ambrose (fourth century) is said to have promoted antiphony in the West, that is to say, the alternation of two choruses that respond to each other. His task of organizing Church music and ridding it of extraneous elements led St. Gregory to establish that tradition definitively in the first of his books, the *Antiphonal*, whereas his second book, the *Cantatorium*, concerns the solo chanting of psalms by the deacon.

Athough there are apparently a great many Gregorian forms, they actually differ more in liturgical significance than in musical configuration. They may be classed under two main headings:

1. The recitative forms: these are the chants that were declaimed *rectotono*, that is, on a single note. This note, which supports every syllable in the text, is, however, bracketed by very short melodic phrases, the *intonatio* (introduction), the *mediatio* (suspension) and the *ponctum* (conclusion). This category includes the *lessons*, *orisons* and *prefaces*, and in general, every type of *intoning*.

2. The melodic forms: here the *melisma* is predominant. The melody starts almost invariably in a low register, blooms into the upper register, and returns to finish on the tonic. Rhythmically, this twofold motion is rendered by a soaring period followed by a moment of repose. Repetitions of phrases, with or without a change of text, are frequent. Thus in the oldest examples the nine *Kyrie* invocations are

arranged in a very simple pattern: AAA, BBB, AAA; later,
however, more complex forms appeared: ABA, CDC, EFE.
To this type belong also the *alleluia*, the *tractus* (a sort of
strophic variation on a melody), the *hymn*, normally divided
into verses and in which the old opposition of long and short
values appears, and the *antiphon*, a kind of refrain grouping
the choruses, and which could also be chanted.

The alleluia was to give birth indirectly to new forms.
Based on an ABA pattern borrowed from the *Kyrie*, it comprises a long central melisma (B) called *jubilus*. In the ninth
century it became customary to adapt a text to this melisma,
one syllable to each note. "This custom soon gave rise to
another, which consisted in paraphrasing religious texts,
sometimes at great length, in developments that were also
sung. These were called the *tropes*. Much of the vocal music
in present-day church service, the *sequences* and *proses*,
were originally tropes on older texts." (Chailley.)

It is somewhat arbitrary to associate the sequent and the
trope with the plain chant: both were already quite a departure from the pure Gregorian tradition.

The Gregorian chant had seriously degenerated as early as
the lower Middle Ages, owing to the loss of its basic traditions. Since the end of the nineteenth century, through the
efforts of the monks of Solesmes, it has recovered what may
be regarded as a substantial share of its original purity. It
remains the epitome of church singing and constitutes the
unalterable foundation of Catholic liturgy.

THE MONODIC CHANSON.

It is difficult, if not impossible, to provide any exact data
concerning the origins of the medieval *chanson*. The most
varied influences probably figured in the struggle that ultimately brought it into being. According to one fairly well-
grounded theory, the influence of church music—Gregorian
plain chant and tropes—was preponderant. Still, we must

not be oversystematic: it may have been the product of constant exchanges between the sacred tradition and the secular repertoire, and not of any unilateral advance.

From the eleventh century on the secular chanson became organized on the artistic level. The trouvères and troubadours invented both the words and the music, improvising an instrumental accompaniment that, we may suppose, hardly differed from the melody. This vocal art, often associated with dancing, developed throughout the twelfth and thirteenth centuries. Its diversity was great: amatory with the *pastourelle*, semi-religious with the *planh*, it could be either aristocratic or popular, and could also take the form of a musical dialogue (*jeu-parti*) closely related to literary genres such as the court romance or miracle play. Later, when the various types of part song came into being and prospered, the monodic song began to decline. Nevertheless the work of the thirteenth-century German *minnesingers*, the bourgeois heirs of the noble troubadours and trouvères, is by no means negligible. From the fourteenth to the seventeenth century the German tradition was perpetuated by generations of *meistersingers* (master singers), the guardians of a rigorously formalistic middle-class art.

The various structures adopted by the monodic song can, according to Th. Gérold, be classed in four principal types: the song without refrain, the song with a different refrain for each stanza, the song with a refrain that stems directly from the melody of the verse (or vice versa), and the song with a fixed structure. This last type includes the *ballette*, out of which came the *ballade*, the *rondel* and the *virelay*, which in turn gave birth to the *rondeau-virelay*.

LITURGICAL AND SECULAR PLAYS.

Out of certain tropes dialogue form was born, beginning in the tenth century. This was an embryonic form of musical drama: the liturgical play (*jeu liturgique*) that developed

during the Middle Ages, ultimately leading to the performances of the Oratorian Brotherhood, which gave birth to the
oratorio. Most of the subjects were biblical. Each episode
gave rise to a melody, sometimes taken up again in another
scene. At times the chorus and soloists were supported by
zithers, viols and harps. The beginnings of the secular
theater are probably not quite so old. The most famous medieval piece, *Le Jeu de Robin et Marion,* by Adam de la
Halle (late thirteenth century), is a kind of dramatic pastourelle that includes five little songs and three short "tunes"
inserted into the dialogue. All were probably sung without
instrumental accompaniment.

THE ORGANUM.

The *organum* or *diaphony* was a compositional technique
that led to the creation of a form. It was the first attempt to
organize a truly polyphonic idiom (ninth century). The
process was necessarily one of trial and error, and the early
organum is primitive and extremely crude. The *vox organalis*
was a kind of counterpoint, grafted note for note onto the
cantus firmus, a type of plain-chant phrase composed of
equal values; their movement was strictly parallel, at an interval of a fourth or a fifth.

A more developed type of diaphony occurred when the
vox organalis was sung in unison at first, then dropped gradually down a fourth and maintained that interval through a
series of parallel movements; at the end of each phrase came
a return to unison. The *vox organalis* was written or, more
commonly, improvised by a cantor. We cannot say positively
whether it was ornamented. Later, a third voice was added,
doubling the *cantus firmus* at the octave; the result was a
polyphony of parallel fifths and fourths, with all the parts
moving on the same rhythm, note against note (Fig. 5).

From the twelfth century on polyphonic writing was en-
riched with a new procedure, the *discant.* Here the *vox*

Fig. 5. Musica enchiriadis: *Organum Rex Celi* (9th century). The *vox organalis* is under the *cantus firmus*.

organalis was replaced by a part called the *discantus* (whence the name of this technique), which differed from it both in position and motion: for indeed the discantus, often improvised, was placed above the cantus firmus, which, in its new bass position, came to be known as the *tenor*. The discantus made a relatively free use of contrary motion, thus putting an end to the obligatory parallelism of the old *organum* and bringing about combinations of alternating unisons, fourths, fifths and octaves. In the thirteenth century incidentals became common in the improvised part. This practice of improvisation in the two-part discant continued to thrive fairly well into the sixteenth century; nevertheless the advance of polyphony, as it established first three- and then four-part techniques of writing, helped gradually to eliminate improvisation from Western musical creation, which became increasingly preconceptional.

In the course of the thirteenth century appeared a new type of organum, which we might call the *free organum*. For it involved considerable freedom of technique and expression, resulting in a polyphonic suppleness that contrasts with the constrained aspect of the primitive organum. The essence of this new organum was its mobility, a *polyphonic* mobility that demanded consonance only at the main harmonic pivots, and a *melodic* mobility, obtained through constant melisma. The *Organum* of Pérotin (beginning of the thirteenth century) is for two, three or four parts. On a "tenor" borrowed from the plain chant but expressed in extremely long values are grafted one, two or three profusely ornamented organum parts.

THE GYMEL.

An isolated form of early English polyphony, the *gymel* differs from the organum in that it utilizes harmonic intervals that are less specifically consonant: the fourth and the fifth were replaced by the third, which the French composers of the day considered dissonant. The gymel was abandoned when the English polyphonists rallied to the Continental concepts, but reappeared in the thirteenth century under the name *faux-bourdon*. In the pieces composed according to this technique the accompanying part was a third lower than the cantus firmus; but tradition held that this part should be sung an octave lower still, so that the thirds became sixths; whence the name "false bass" (*falso bordone*). The faux-bourdon, in the fifteenth century, brought vigor to the second period of the Ars Nova, opening the way for a truly harmonic idiom.

THE CONDUCTUS.

In the twelfth and thirteenth centuries the name *conductus* was given to every polyphonic vocal composition written in the manner of the organum, that is to say, note against note, but in which the tenor, instead of being borrowed from Gregorian sources, was composed in a free style. This made it possible to write two-, three-, and four-part *conducti* that departed from the liturgical repertoire. This type of writing was taken up again in several secular forms, notably the rondo.

THE MEDIEVAL MOTET.

Originally a liturgical form, the *motet* (from the Latin *motetus*, "word") has had a strange destiny. It grew from an attempt to enrich the conductus and the organum by the trope: taking as their point of departure the discant principle of superimposing several different melodies, a number of polyphonists of St. Louis' day conceived the idea of setting different words to each part. At the end of the thirteenth century the motet appears as a curious synthesis of sacred and profane elements; one, two or three parts are set against a liturgical cantus firmus, each carrying a different text (written, at times, in the vernacular), one word for each note. In many instances the refrain of a rondo was even added, with words of an amatory nature (*motet ente*). Often the cantus firmus or tenor was played by an instrument. This form, quite hybrid liturgically, is of tremendous musical interest; it was the first attempt to liberate rhythm in a polyphonic context: for the first time the voices stopped singing note against note. The *isorhythmic* motets* of Philippe de Vitry and Guillaume de Machaut were an attempt to unify musical discourse through rhythm, an idea not taken up again until the twentieth century (Stravinsky, Messiaen, Boulez).

In the fourteenth century the commonest form of motet called for instruments. In general, only the upper part was sung, so that once again the form fitted into a liturgical category. The instrumental prelude, interlude and postlude made only a relatively brief appearance: the fifteenth century was to be the age of *a cappella* vocal polyphony, with the extraordinary achievements of the Franco-Flemish school in this form. (See *Motet.*)

THE MASS.

The *mass* is much too important a form to be dealt with in the framework of medieval music, for it overlaps many different periods. At this point we shall merely remind the reader that in the Middle Ages it took two opposite forms:

* Isorhythm is the application of a single rhythmic design to different melodic patterns.

on the one hand, the Gregorian mass, which was strictly monodic, and on the other, the polyphonic mass, which was first fragmentary but was unified in the fourteenth century by Guillaume de Machaut. (See *Mass*.)

THE RONDEAU OR VIRELAY.

The medieval *rondeau* is a vocal form, a kind of dance or round sung in alternation, the voice alone for the verse, the chorus for the refrain. It was of real importance in the development of polyphonic music, especially starting with Adam de la Halle (thirteenth century), whose three-part rondeaus, written note-against-note in the style of the conductus, have rightly remained famous. The eight verses of the rondeau were ordinarily divided between two melodic designs, according to the pattern aba' aa" ab; sometimes a and b were used for several verses. The rondeau of the fifteenth century, more commonly called *virelay*, had an instrumental accompaniment. It was the most widespread song form in France during the Ars Nova era; Dufay and Binchois left many examples of it. The *rode* was another form of rondo, which borrowed from the Florentine *caccia* a technique of composition in three parts, two in canon form. The rondeau disappeared about the beginning of the sixteenth century. A hundred years later the French lutists and harpsichordists were to provide it with a fruitful posterity in the field of purely instrumental music.

THE LAY.

The *lay* is a vocal piece with instrumental accompaniment; or, more rarely, a purely instrumental piece. Its origins are uncertain. Many pieces described by their composers as lays were merely ordinary chansons; in the work of Guillaume de Machaut, the master of this form, the lay is a sizable vocal composition, in twelve stanzas, of which only the last melodically repeats the first.

THE LAUDE.

In the thirteenth and fourteenth centuries it was common to sing *laudes*—a kind of pious hymn sung in the vernacular—in Italian religious processions. These songs of praise, almost always anonymous, were at first monodic. Even when they became polyphonic, they still kept a very rudimentary technique, characterized by syllabic writing, note against note, and a highly symmetrical structure. The laude may have influenced the beginnings of the chorale and the oratorio.

THE CANON.

The *canon* is a compositional device from which the fourteenth-century Italians created a form, called *fuga* (from the verb *fugare*, "to flee")—not to be confused with the classical fugue—or *caccia* ("chase"). As a technical device the canon is characterized by the pursuit of a single melodic phrase with two or more voices entering one after the other. We therefore deal here with contrapuntal imitation, such as is found in all polyphonic music to the time of Bach, but in the strictest form, according to its most rigid rule (its canon).

There are many kinds of canons. In the canons called "two in one" and "two in one at the octave" the part that first introduces the melodic pattern, called the *antecedent*, is imitated from beginning to end, note for note, by the second part, or *consequent*. In the canon of "two in one at the fifth below" the consequent reproduces the same rhythm and intervals as those expressed by the antecedent, only a fifth lower. Canons may be written at every interval.

In the canon by augmentation the note values introduced

by the antecedent are doubled in the counter-subject, quarter notes becoming half notes and half notes whole notes. The reverse holds for the canon by diminution. The canon by contrary motion, in which all melodically ascending motion becomes descending, and vice versa (Fig. 6), differs from

Fig. 6. *The Musical Offering* (J. S. Bach). Two-part canon. The consequent strictly imitates the antecedent by contrary motion.

the retrograde canon (also called "crab canon") in which the last note of the antecedent becomes the first note of the consequent, so that it comes out as if one were reading the antecedent in a mirror. A fourth type results from the combination of *contrary* and *retrograde* motion.

The *caccia* and *fuga*, small two-part vocal pieces with instrumental accompaniment, appeared in the fourteenth century in the work of the first Florentine masters; however, undoubtedly the canon already existed in folk music. The oldest known canon comes from the English school of the thirteenth century. However, the English *catch* and the French *rode* are merely adaptations of the Italian caccia. Soon the art of the canon was also exploited, in the richer framework of the motet form, by the composers of the Franco-Flemish school. It reached its greatest height at the end of the fifteenth century, with Ockeghem, author of the famous *Deo Gratias*, a nonuple canon in thirty-six parts. Subsequently, although the form itself disappeared, the canon technique continued to contribute intermittently to the development of polyphonic music. A number of modern composers (Messiaen) have even used an ingenious new device known as *rhythmic canon*.

THE FLORENTINE MADRIGAL.

The *madrigal* was, along with the caccia, the favorite form of the masters of the Florentine Ars Nova. It first made its appearance at the end of the thirteenth century, that is, at the time of Dante and Petrarch; Pietro Casella, a friend of Dante, is said to have invented it. It consisted of a song for one voice with an instrumental accompaniment that also supplied interludes and a postlude. Its style was suppler, its melody more ornate, its text more refined and delicate than those of its contemporary, the French rondeau. The Florentine madrigal flourished in the fourteenth century with masters like Jacopo da Bologna and Francesco Landino. In the fifteenth century the more popular style of the *frottola* superseded it throughout northern Italy. However, the influence of Florentine songs on the Ars Nova movement as a whole was very fruitful indeed.

THE MEDIEVAL BALLAD.

Like the French rondeau, the Florentine madrigal and the Italian frottola, the Spanish and French *ballads* of the fourteenth and fifteenth centuries are accompanied art songs; they differ from those other forms by their style and structure. The ballad derived from a stylization of the dance tunes frequent among the trouvères and troubadours of the twelfth and thirteenth centuries. Toward the end of the fifteenth century it was replaced by the polyphonic chanson and by instrumental dance music.

The structure of the Spanish ballad involves a kind of refrain, the *ripresa*, which is sung in chorus at the beginning and the end of the work, a double verse, or *piedi* and a *false refrain*, the *volta*, that uses different words with the music of the ripresa. In the French ballads of the time of Dufay the last verse is used for the refrain and there is no initial ripresa.

THE FROTTOLA.

The *frottola*, very popular in fifeenth-century northern
Italy, presents close analogies with the Florentine madrigal,
from which it derives, and with its contemporary, the ballad.
However, its style is definitely more popular, the words
(often full of onomatopoeia) are more crude and the structure is very simple. It was written in four parts, note against
note, but only the upper part was sung, the other parts being
played on instruments. The text is divided into stanzas, each
stanza comprised of eight-syllable lines. The music consists of
two phrases, each of which encompasses two lines of verse,
with the first being repeated three times. (AAAB). Among
the principal composers of the frottola were Marco Cara and
Bartolomeo Tromboncino. Although the form survived until
the sixteenth century, it was gradually absorbed by the infinitely richer Italian madrigal and by the *villanelle*, whose
simple style was much more to the people's taste.

THE VILLANELLE.

The *villanelle* or *canzoneta* was a popular vocal form.
More precisely, it was one of the most common forms in
Italian folk music in the fifteenth century. It was written for
several parts; but its texture and structure alike were very
rudimentary. Like the frottola, with which it has certain
features in common, especially its light, deliberately comical
character, it is strictly homophonic. Its style, however, is less
refined. It gradually disappeared in the course of the sixteenth century.

MINUET

The *minuet* is a French dance; it was very fashionable in aristocratic circles under the reigns of Louis XIV and Louis XV, despite its folk origin. (In sixteenth-century Poitou the minuet was a variety of the *branle*.) Toward the end of the eighteenth century it became an instrumental form of no mean importance, as part of the classical symphony (Stamitz, Haydn, Mozart). Before that it was found in the suite, holding the same optional position as the *gavotte*, the *passepied* and the *forlane*, and in the ballets of French opera (Lully and his successors). It was then a dance in three-part time, simply written, but sometimes preciously. At first the minuet's tempo was quite leisurely, but from the time of its inclusion in the symphony it grew increasingly faster until it finally led up to the Beethoven scherzo, which took its place. Hardly any minuets have been written since the end of the eighteenth century.

STRUCTURE.

The minuet comprises two distinct pieces, played without a pause and followed by a da capo (ABA), the first piece (A) being repeated in toto at the end of the second piece (B). The latter is the so-called second minuet, or *trio* (in contrast with the first piece, ordinarily played by the entire orchestra, the trio was almost always for soloists: two violins and a viola, or two oboes and a bassoon); it has the same construction as the first, but differs in the nature of its theme, which is usually more melodic, and often also in its key, which may be either the relative or the dominant of the principal key. In the seventeenth century and at the beginning of the eighteenth, the structure of both pieces, the first minuet and the trio, was the same as that adopted in the various dance sections of the suite, i.e., the *binary form.* (See *Suite.*) The double minuet of J. S. Bach's First Suite for Orchestra, for example, is constructed exactly like the other movements. However, during the second period of the minuet, that of *le style galant*, the influence of the sonata form produced a "ternary" construction. The first minuet of Mozart's Sonata in A major for piano is constructed as a kind of short sonata allegro—it even contains the suggestion of a second theme—in which the central modulating section is based on a new element. The re-entry of the principal theme in the initial key may be regarded as a sonata-type re-exposition. The trio that follows is in the subdominant (a custom that has been kept alive in military marches, the structure of which is a simplification of the minuet) and monothematic, despite the use of a secondary design in the middle section; with this exception its structure is identical with that of the first minuet.

MOTET

The *motet* is a vocal piece, essentially liturgical, designed to illustrate the prayers of a church service.*

In the course of the fifteenth century the medieval motet

* Other pieces with the same general purpose are often identified with the motet: responses, hymns, laments, litanies and *Magnificat* verses.

(see *Medieval Forms*) gave way to a new form, of considerable historical importance. Indeed the *a cappella* motet in imitative style—admirable examples of which were produced by the Franco-Flemish school (Josquin, Lassus) and the school of Rome (Palestrina, Victoria)—gave birth to a great variety of forms, from the vocal mass to the instrumental ricercare.

In the seventeenth century, under the influence of the new ideas, the Italian motet evolved in the direction of a resolutely monodic style, in which solo voices (usually one or two) are supported either by a simple *basso continuo* or by the orchestra (Monteverdi, Carissimi, Schütz, Legrenzi). At the same time there were even instances in which the hint of a dramatic action made its appearance, so that the form tended to become identified with the church cantata, then in its infancy. The composition was divided into fragments and began to acquire sizable dimensions. By the end of the century the motet, like the cantata, was filled with recitatives, arias, duets and trios. The French motet, from Lully to La Lande, takes the same form. Finally, about 1720, Bach provided the masterpiece of the cantata-motet with his *Magnificat*;* a bit later, with his great *a cappella* motets for double chorus, he attained the summit of religious musical expression. After that the motet in all its aspects underwent a decline that seems to have been interrupted by no subsequent work of genius. (See *Cantata; Anthem; Psalm.*)

STRUCTURE.

The *a cappella* motet, generally written for four or five voices, is based on a Latin text taken from a church service. Indeed, among the polyphonists of the Franco-Flemish school and the Roman school the text determined the musical structure of the composition. To each phrase or meaning-

* Liturgically, the *Magnificat*, a hymn to the Virgin, cannot be considered a motet, but musically it seems proper to include it in this form.

ful fragment of a phrase there corresponds a freely invented melodic phrase sung by each of the parts in turn, according to the method of contrapuntal imitation in vogue among the polyphonists of that period. The result is a series of episodes that, aside from the text itself, are linked only by their construction on the same scale and in the same style, and the fact that they overlap. It is, in short, the procedure of the mass, except that here no generating theme is introduced. In this case the only source of unity is the absolute equality of the parts; no one is subordinated to its neighbor, whether bass or soprano (Fig. 7).

The duplex motet is most often written for four parts. It comprises a series of fugal expositions (one to each phrase) in which the voices enter two by two, the principal melodic design being accompanied by a counter-subject (Victoria's *Duo seraphin clamabant*).

The *responses* are usually grouped in three. Each of the three sections is itself divided in two parts, the *response* proper and the *verse*, both of which end on the same prayer. More than the motet itself, the response gave rise to homophonic expositions in which the chromaticism of the madrigal sometimes found a place (*Piange quasi virgo*, by Palestrina).

Sometimes the motet adopted the structure of the response (*O vos omnes*, by Victoria); this is why I felt the two forms should be dealt with in the same chapter, for independently of their liturgical significance they are really the same form.

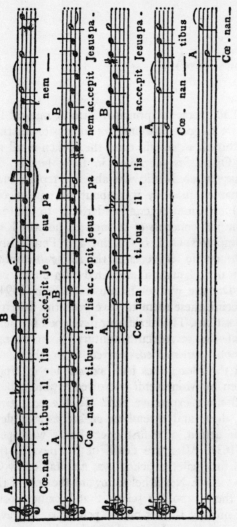

Fig. 7. Motet *Coenantibus illis* (Palestrina).

OPERA

The opera, the principal form of musical theater, is a large-scale tragedy or drama set to music. All the roles are sung, although in certain cases the spoken word may be introduced. Opera first appeared in Italy, late in the sixteenth century, when tonality was about to replace modality, and accompanied monody was about to replace counterpoint. A Florentine coterie undertook to restore the dramatico-musical concepts of antiquity. The poet Rinuccini and the composers Galilei, Caccini and Peri, wishing to bring out the poetic text, created the *stilo representativo,* a sort of musical declamation supported by a *basso continuo.* Rinuccini's *Daphne* was set to music by Peri (1594), and later by Caccini; these seem to have been the first true dramatic compositions. The movement developed further at the beginning of the seventeenth century. Soon opera, then called *dramma per musica,* strayed from the somewhat ascetic path the Florentines had laid out for it. Under the impetus given by Monteverdi it evolved toward a better organized and more expressive style. To the recitative were added arias, duets and ensembles; an orchestra underscored the dramatic action. The first opera house was opened in Venice in 1637. After the death of Monteverdi the preeminence of the Venetian school was maintained by Cavalli, Legranzi and Costi. Nevertheless toward the end of the century it was the Neapolitan school that became most representative of musical theater on the peninsula. However, this Neapolitan supremacy, despite the undeniable stature of the prolific Alessandro Scarlatti, coincided with a certain deca-

dence of Italian opera. In a scant century it had been radically diverted from its original principles; dramatic action
was reduced to a minimum, the poetic text was sacrificed to
bel canto; only the singer and his vocal effects mattered.
During the same period French opera cleaved much closer to
the line of Monteverdi and the Florentines: Lully and his
successors made this one of the most brilliant periods in the
history of French musical drama, culminating in the masterpieces of Rameau. In England Purcell's admirable *Dido and
Aeneas* (1689) was an attempt to create a specifically English form of opera, but as such it was a dead end: at the
beginning of the eighteenth century Italian opera, as represented by Bononcini and Handel, conquered the London
public completely. In Germany Schütz, imitating the Florentines, put on his *Daphne* in 1627, but not until 1678 did a
public opera house open in Hamburg, which for more than
half a century remained the capital of German opera. Keiser,
Kusser, Mattheson and Telemann shared the programs with
the Italian authors who had provided their inspiration.

In the first half of the eighteenth century *opera buffa* (see
Light Opera) appeared; it soon brought fresh blood to Italian opera and gave birth to the French *opéra-comique*.
However, *opera seria*, or grand opera, did not immediately
drop from public favor in Italy. The most popular composers were the German Hasse and the Italians Bononcini,
Porpora, Jomelli and Piccini. Piccini was held up as an example against Gluck in France. Nevertheless Gluck suc-
ceeded in carrying out worthwhile reforms in grand opera,
restoring the importance of dramatic values and reducing to
its proper place the role of *bel canto*. This reform made
Paris the center of musical drama; the Italians themselves
went there for recognition (Cherubini, Spontini, Bellini and
Rossini). This did not prevent the French school proper
from entering into an unfortunate eclipse: not a single figure
stands out between Rameau and Berlioz. On the other hand,

Mozart was giving the German school its first great operatic masterpieces.

During the nineteenth century traditional opera, with its arias, recitatives and ariosi, disappeared. While the decline of Italian opera was well under way, German opera was getting a completely new lease on life, in form and spirit, first with Weber, then with Richard Wagner, whose musical dramas brought a new interdependence between drama and music. The Russian school, influenced first by the Italians, reached the loftiest peaks of a typically Slavic art in Mussorgsky's *Boris Godunov*. After producing a few scores toward the end of the century that attested evident recovery, the French school inaugurated the twentieth century with a veritable bombshell: Claude Debussy's *Pelléas*. However, this appears to have been an exceptional and isolated achievement. Somehow the twentieth century does not seem likely to be a great period of musical drama. Our contemporary sensibilities may be unreceptive to the conventions of a genre many consider outdated. Few masterpieces have appeared to contradict this apparent condemnation. There is, however, that masterpiece of German expressionism, Berg's *Wozzeck*, composed just after World War I.

STRUCTURE.

The structure of an opera is determined by its *libretto*.* According to the number of characters on stage and the action assigned them in the libretto, the musical score takes the form of recitative, arioso, aria, duet or chorus. This enumeration alone makes it clear that opera is like cantata in that it is a composite form, and it is built from the same simple forms. However, since its dramatic action is more sustained, the recitative and the arioso are undoubtedly more important.

* Obviously this statement can also be applied to other dramatic or semi-dramatic forms, such as the ballet, the cantata and the oratorio.

Any opera's overall structure belongs to one of the following types:

1. The old type, or "opera in set pieces," in which each "number" constitutes an entity, clearly separated from those that precede and follow it. It may be useful to set forth the plan of the first act of Mozart's *Don Giovanni*. For *Don Giovanni*, despite lying between opera and *opera buffa,* is an excellent example of the construction in set pieces:

1. Introduction (ensemble)	Leporello, Donna Anna, Don Giovanni, the Commander
2. Recitative and duet	Donna Anna and Ottavio
3. Trio	Donna Elvira, Don Giovanni, Leporello
4. Aria	Leporello
5. Duet and Chorus	Zerlina, Mazetto, peasants
6. Aria	Mazetto
7. Duet	Don Giovanni, Zerlina
8. Aria	Donna Elvira
9. Quartet	Donna Elvira, Donna Anna, Ottavio, Don Giovanni
10. Recitative and Air	Donna Anna
11. Aria	Ottavio
12. Aria	Don Giovanni
13. Aria	Zerlina
14. Finale (ensemble)	The entire cast

Note that each number is separated from the next by a *recitativo secco,* during which the action progresses. This purely Italian type of recitative is replaced in French opera (e.g., Rameau) by the somewhat heavier *recitative libre.*

2. The modern type, or lyric drama, in which the unit of construction is no longer the set piece but rather the scene.

Here dramatic continuity is preserved more rigorously, through the constant interlocking of the various musical phases. Consequently these are much less clearly differentiated than in the old type opera. As we have seen, with Wagner the aria became a sort of arioso, soaring above an extremely dense, continuous orchestral fabric, itself illuminated—according to the dramatic plan—by the use of the *leitmotif* (a musical motif symbolizing an idea or person). With Debussy a new kind of recitative, particularly flexible and melodic, was substituted for the traditional forms. *Pelléas et Mélisande* contains no arias, no duets, no chorus. The only divisions in the work are those provided by the orchestral interludes to separate the tableaux.

OPERETTA

Operetta arose from *opéra-comique* in the mid-nineteenth century and differs from it essentially by the lightness of its subject and by its style.

Spoken passages are more frequent, and the music is confined on the whole to a series of tunes framed in a few ensembles, here and there discreetly accompanied by the orchestra. When light opera composers began to treat subjects previously reserved for grand opera in its present form operetta developed as a reaction and became crystallized in its present form. However, operetta belongs to a long tradition that goes back to the Italian *opera buffa* of the eighteenth century, the *intermezzo* and *mascarade* of the sixteenth and seventeenth centuries, and even to such medieval plays as the *Jeu de Robin et Marion*, by Adam de la Halle (thirteenth century). Hervé, Offenbach, Lecocq, Planquette and Johann Strauss in the nineteenth century, and Messagier in the twentieth, have written many unpretentious pages that contain more music than many of the grand operas of the same era.

ORATORIO

The *oratorio* is a sort of grand-scale cantata, often involving many characters. Its origins are in the liturgical plays and mysteries that St. Philip of Neri's Society of Oratorians (sixteenth century) presented to the Roman public. Cavalieri's *Anima e Corpo* (1600) is regarded as one of the earliest examples. The form may at first have been exclusively theatrical. Carissimi, in the mid-seventeenth century, may have introduced the narrator, thereby steering the oratorio toward the concert hall. In any case, the form reached its high point at the end of the seventeenth and during the first half of the eighteenth century in France, with M.-A. Charpentier's *Histoires Sacrées*; in Germany and in England with, above all, Bach's *Passions* (q.v.) and Handel's biblical oratorios.

Haydn's *The Seasons* marks the expansion of the oratorio into the world of secular music. Despite a few lovely pages by Berlioz, Liszt and Franck, the nineteenth century was a period of decline. There was a sort of revival after World War I, notably by Honegger and Milhaud.

STRUCTURE.

Like the cantata, the oratorio is a composite form, and contains the same elements: arias, ariosos, recitatives, duets, trios and choruses. However, the role of the orchestra is distinctly more important: at times long, expressive interludes are entrusted to it (*The Pastoral Symphony* in *The Messiah*).

Handel's *Messiah*, the archetype of the seventeenth-century oratorio, recounts the life of Christ in three parts; it has seven recitatives, seventeen arias and seventeen choruses. In some of his oratorios Handel used only the chorus, alternating fugal and homophonic writing. Among the moderns the narrator's role is generally spoken rather than sung (*La Danse des Morts*, by Honegger); this is true also of the many characters who people the vast fresco of *Jeanne au bucher*, also by Honegger, which contains the most disparate musical elements: folk songs, chorales, dance tunes, symphonic pieces and choruses in a series of scenes that follow one another in the style of modern opera, in contrast with the "set pieces" of the old-fashioned oratorio.

OVERTURE

The *overture*, traditionally conceived for orchestra, is a composition, of varying length and development, that constitutes the opening of most operas and oratorios, as well as some instrumental suites. The oldest known example is the toccata for trombones and organ that precedes Monteverdi's *Orfeo* (1608). In the seventeenth century it became the custom to begin an opera with a short canzone or sinfonia: this was known as the "overture in the Italian style." The "overture in the French style," already a part of the *ballet de cour,* but which Lully soon made popular all over Europe (Italy excepted), long remained a much richer form. It gave its name to the French suite (see *Suite*), of which it constitutes the introductory piece, and occasionally to the German suite: Bach called his famous orchestral suites *overtures.* The term was even extended to include the harpsichord suite. Toward the middle of the eighteenth century, however, the French overture came to be considered outdated, while the Italian overture, receiving an extraordinary impetus from composers like Handel, Hasse, Galuppi and Jonelli, came to the fore. Subsequently the overture underwent the influence of the classical symphony, adopting both the style and the structure of the latter's initial allegro (Mozart). In the nineteenth century the potpourri type of overture was introduced, in which the principal airs of the opera are set forth one after another (Rossini). Then came Wagner's symphonic prologue, conceived in a spirit close to that of the symphonic poem; this, like the Mozart overture, can stand as an independent work, and indeed, concert performances of such overtures are quite common. In the twentieth century operas and oratorios alike seem to do without overtures, usually replacing them with short orchestral introductions (Debussy's *Pelléas and Mélisande*), which sometimes amount to only a few measures (Berg's *Wozzeck*).

STRUCTURE.

The structure of the overture varies with the type adopted. The Italian overture—as it appears in the work of Alessandro Scarlatti, for example—comprises two rapid movements separated by a slow movement: all three are played without interruption.

Lully's French overture is in three parts, but here two

slow movements (*graves*) are separated by a fast movement. The *graves* are written for five parts—possibly a reminiscence of the expressive madrigal—and in a rhythm in which dotted notes predominate. It is rare for the second *grave* to literally repeat the first. The central movement is often in fugue style. Bach placed this type overture at the beginning of his four *Suites* for orchestra.

Rameau altered the French overture by doing away with the second *grave*. The initial slow movement works its way toward the dominant, while the fast movement works its way back to the tonic.

The classical overture also involved a slow introduction, but from Mozart on this tended to grow shorter, and the main interest was concentrated in the allegro, which borrowed its tonal pattern from the sonata (*Don Giovanni*). However, at times there is a central episode that emphasizes elements not contained in the exposition (*The Magic Flute*).

The types of overture in vogue during the second half of the nineteenth century were more closely bound up with the style of the main work. The potpourri overture (*Carmen*) sums up the principal airs of the score, linked rather rudimentarily. The Wagnerian prelude (*Lohengrin, Parsifal*) is more carefully constructed and evokes with greater subtlety the drama's atmosphere. In the modern opera this prelude is sometimes reduced to the dimensions of the introduction in the classical overture; but in compensation the number of interludes between the scenes is increased (*Pelléas*).

PASSACAGLIA

The *passacaglia* was originally a tenth-century marching tune that later became a slow dance in triple time. In the seventeenth and eighteenth centuries it gained its full importance as a form of instrumental music. Occasionally it was incorporated into a suite, as the final and most extensively developed section. The classics and romantics completely abandoned this form, which thus far has made only rare appearances in contemporary music (*Wozzeck*).

STRUCTURE.

The passacaglia, a composition in the polyphonic style, offers genuine analogies with the *chaconne* and the *ground* (q.v.): all these forms are based on a design, the repetition of which gives rise to variations either in the statement of the theme or in the other parts. The principle of the passacaglia is that the generative pattern, whether it remains in the bass, or, as is less frequent, moves into the other parts, remains intact throughout most of the variations. Therefore the other parts must carry such fresh developments as are indispensable to the progress of the work. This is true of Bach's *Passacaglia and Fugue* for organ, which polyphonically is the richest piece of music ever written on the principle of the ground bass. The statement of the theme—a very simple melody, the opening notes of which were borrowed from a seventeenth-century French composer, André Raison—is followed by twenty variations, each involving a combination of the theme with a different secondary motif. The theme is presented in its entirety in fifteen of the twenty variations; it is altered rhythmically according to the configuration of the secondary motifs that accompany it in variations 5, 9 and 13; it appears in the "soprano" part in variations 11 and 12; in the "alto" in variation 13; and it is barely indicated, in the bass, in variations 14 and 15. (See V*ariation*).

The *Fugue,* which follows the *Passacaglia,* is written on the same subject. It is interesting to note, vis-à-vis tonal construction, that the structure of the passacaglia and, more generally, of the ground bass technique, is something of a hindrance to modulation: the entry of the answer (the subject being taken up in the dominant key) in the fifth measure of the *Fugue* introduces a new key for the first time in this relatively long composition, for we cannot properly consider true modulations the occasional "borrowings" through which Bach endeavors to mitigate the static tonal pattern imposed on him by his theme.

PASSION

The *Passion* is not a well-defined form: sometimes related to the motet, sometimes to the oratorio, it differs from both by its quasi-dramatic spirit, with theatrical lyricism and church style balancing each other. Dramatically, it tells the story of the Passion of Christ according to the Gospels, as prescribed by the ritual of Holy Week. As early as the Middle Ages it was the custom to divide among several cantors the voices of Jesus, Pilate, Judas and so on. About 1600, in Italy, the recitative style appeared in sacred plays. The Passion became a sort of motet with many characters, a cantata without orchestra. This form reached its full development in Germany with Schütz and Sebastiani (seventeenth century), who incorporated the Protestant chorale; then came Telemann, Handel and Bach, who treated the Passion as a vast oratorio. The decline sacred music has undergone since the second half of the eighteenth century is particularly noticeable here: not since the cantor of Leipzig has a single composer written a Passion of any significance.

STRUCTURE.

Although its size is certainly larger, structurally the eighteenth-century Passion is identical with the oratorio or the cantata. In Bach's *Passions* we find again the recitative, pure or accompanied (the solo part here personifies the Evangelist), the arioso, the aria, the chorus and the chorale, harmonized or figured; they follow one another in an immense fresco of seventy-eight pieces. The earlier Passions involved only a few of these elements: with Schütz recitatives alternate with chorales; still more sparing are the partly chanted Passions of the sixteenth century (Victoria, Byrd), where the emphasis is placed on the recto tono recitation of the text.

POLYPHONIC CHANSON

The polyphonic song (*chanson*) is one of the basic forms of the sixteenth-century Franco-Flemish school. It sprang from the marriage of the folk spirit of the monodic

chanson with the learned language of the contrapuntal motet
in imitations. Like its contemporary, the Italian madrigal, it
is meant to be sung *a cappella*. The number of parts seems
to have been quite variable, for whereas the usual scoring
called for four parts, there are many examples of three- , five-
and six-part scores. The character of the polyphonic
chanson was equally varied: alongside the picturesque compositions of Janequin, or the risqué texts set to music by
Lassus or Costeley, we sometimes find a song by Josquin des
Prés that expresses intense pathos.

STRUCTURE.

The polyphonic chanson has no well-defined structure. It
often borrows the verse-refrain alternation that is the common trait of the rondeau, the virelay and the medieval ballad
from which it derived. However, this alternation can assume
many aspects. In *La Plus Belle de La Ville* by Janequin, the
refrain is identical each time, both in words and music,
whereas in each of the three verses the same music is repeated but with different words. In *Le Chant des Oiseaux*,
also by Janequin, each repetition of the refrain involves new
words, requiring changes in the music, and each new verse
differs from the preceding one in its most humorous part,
made up of onomatopoeic words of all kinds (this composition is one of the oldest known examples of descriptive
music).

Among the common patterns we shall cite one derived
from the motet: each phrase has a different melodic pattern,
taken up by each of the voices in turn in canonic imitation.
However, this method is never applied as rigorously in the
polyphonic chanson as in the motet; thus certain songs by
Roland de Lassus use it in opposition to homophonic passages designed to provide a contrast (*Soyons joyeux sur la
plaisante verdure*). Others use it more systematically: con-
tinuously introducing new motifs, they proceed from begin-

ning to end without a single repeat, not even a partial
reference to the opening section (*Las, voulez-vous qu'une
personne chante*).

Related to this last structure, the freest of all, are those in
which the first or the first two musical phrases are repeated,
but with a different text, while the end of the song is allowed
to develop freely (*Quand mon mari vient de dehors*, by
Lassus). A song like Costeley's *Mignonne, allons voir si la
rose* uses a more subtle construction: at first view it appears
made up of a three-part verse and a four-part refrain repeated twice in order, with different words; but closer examination shows that the repeat is not taken note for note:
besides being recognizably condensed (twenty-four measures
instead of forty), the last part contains appreciable melodic
changes that considerably alter it, even though this second
passage for four voices unquestionably derives from the first.
Both are strictly homophonic compositions, whereas the
passages for three voices are contrapuntal. Less frequently
we come across a completely homophonic chanson (*Las,
viens moi secourir*, by Janequin).

PRELUDE

The *prelude* belongs essentially to instrumental
music. Its dimensions are quite variable, and as its name
indicates, its function is to introduce one or more other
pieces: a fugue or a suite of dances. However, some composers, like Chopin and Debussy, have written series of
preludes that stand alone. Although certain organ pieces—in
for example, Ileborgh's tablatures (1448)—are entitled
preludia, the prelude originated in sixteenth-century lute

music. The Italians gave the name *intonazione* to the few
phrases the instrumentalist improvised before performing a
musical selection, thereby establishing the composition's
key, and at the same time making sure his instrument was
tuned. As it was handed down from the lute to the harpsichord and the organ in the seventeenth century, the into
nazione became the prelude, which grew steadily in importance right up to Bach. All the leading English, German and
French polyphonists cultivated this form. (See *Fantasy;*
Toccata; Overture.)

STRUCTURE.

In the seventeenth century the prelude was a very free
form: even when written out it suggested an improvisational
style. Among the French masters of the period (Louis
Couperin, Lebègue) it was not even divided into measures.
It was merely a succession of phrases linked only by the key
signature (a reminder of its origins). As such it presented
certain affinities with the fantasy, and especially with the
toccata. (See *Fantasy* and *Toccata.*)

J. S. Bach was one of the very first to think of organizing
the prelude, endowing it with far greater dimensions and a
firm structure. His harpsichord and organ music contains a
great variety of preludes. The most widely known is undoubtedly the prelude *in bicinium* (invertible two-part counterpoint), in which the thematic elements stated in the bass
are conceived so that they may shift into the upper part, and
vice versa. This form of prelude often borrows its binary
structure from the movements of the suite (*Well-Tempered*
Clavichord, Book II, No. 20). Another frequent type is the
prelude for two or three parts, in imitative style (Book II,
No. 9). A third type is closer to the toccata in that it, too,
uses a more specifically harmonic style of writing, in which
virtuoso effects are not infrequent (Book I, No. 21); in
other instances, on the contrary, the composer weaves

harmonic developments on a simple design in the form of an arpeggio (Book I, No. 1). More rarely, the prelude borrows the structure of the French overture or the Italian sinfonia. Large-scale constructions are ordinarily reserved for the organ preludes, built on one or two themes (the famous Prelude in E flat involves three themes). We would therefore be tempted to write that Bach had exhausted this form, had not the prelude been undeniably given a new lease on life by certain nineteenth- and twentieth-century masters. However, this revival was essentially one of style: Chopin's and Debussy's preludes, admirable though they are from the expressive standpoint, offer little architectonic interest.

PSALM

The *psalm* is one of the least well-defined vocal forms. It is a song of praise handed down from the Hebrew religion to the Catholic liturgy, and thence to the Protestant church service. St. Ambrose seems to have borrowed its original form, involving two alternating choruses, from the Orthodox church. Over the centuries the psalm has undergone many transformations. It was first adopted by the Gregorian plain chant; then the first polyphonists treated it in the organum form (twelfth and thirteenth centuries). In the fourteenth century it was commonly sung by one voice with instrumental accompaniment. It was the most current vocal form in the French Reformation. Gondimel and Claude le Jeune wrote psalms for four parts (sometimes more), *a cappella*, in a highly syllabic style. In seventeenth-century France the psalm took on the general outlines of the cantata and the *grand motet,* with choruses, soloists and orchestra (*De Profundis,* by De Lalande). This tradition of the large-scale psalm with orchestra has produced a number of modern compositions like the *Psaume* by Florent Schitt and Stravinsky's *Symphony of Psalms.*

QUARTET

The *quartet* is an instrumental or vocal composition written for four parts. It does not follow that every composition written for four parts is a quartet in the full meaning of the term: in fact since the fifteenth century four-part composition, which makes it possible to combine richness and simplicity, has been the type of writing most frequently employed in every genre. From that period on masses, motets and polyphonic chansons were often written for four parts. At the end of the sixteenth century composition in five and more parts was developed; in the seventeenth century, on the contrary, the trio forms seem to have predominated; however, four-part composition held its own. About the middle of the eighteenth century the string section, which included two violin parts, one viola part and one cello part (doubled in the orchestra by the contrabass), was the principal nucleus of the embryonic symphony orchestra. As instruments tended to become individualized, the string section gradually freed itself until it formed an independent whole, both as an ensemble and as a form. Although Boccherini's first quartets were little more than symphonies for strings, Stamitz and Gossec were already differentiating between those of their quartets to be played on four instruments and those to be played by the orchestra. The influence of the *divertimento*, by introducing small ensembles of soloists, established the string quartet definitively. Starting with Haydn and Mozart, the string quartet became the principal form of chamber music, along with the sonata. From Beethoven to Bela Bartok nearly all the great musicians have favored it.

Other types of quartet have come into use, especially since the beginning of the nineteenth century. Most common is the piano quartet, composed of a piano and a string trio.

Aside from the instrumental quartet, we should mention the vocal quartet, although it is more a combination of sonorities than a true musical form. Normally the four parts of a vocal quartet correspond to the four main types of human voice: soprano, contralto, tenor and bass. However, other combinations are also possible; one of the most common is the male quartet, involving two tenors, a baritone and a bass. The vocal quartet is the basic arrangement of all the major choral forms, except for the madrigal.

STRUCTURE.

The instrumental quartet has no specific structure; like all the classical forms of chamber music, it borrows that of the sonata. However, it seldom comprises less than four movements, and some of Beethoven's quartets contain even more (Fourteenth Quartet).

RECITATIVE

In the *recitative* the musical phrase is strictly subservient to the language, closely following the rhythm of the words, emphasizing at times their accentuation rather than their meaning. This form came into being with opera, and is one of its chief components. Like opera, it was first developed by the sixteenth-century Florentines (Peri, Gaccini, Galilei), who felt that their most urgent task was to restore the predominance in vocal music of the poetic text, to which the complexities of contrapuntal writing were so detrimental.

At first the recitative was accompanied only by a simple instrumental *basso continuo*, designed to keep the pitch. A great deal of freedom was left to the singer, and the instrumental accompaniment, which amounted to a few chords here and there, was not an element of constraint. However, the use of rhymed texts inevitably led the composers back to a more melodically and rhythmically controlled form of music. Thus there appeared, in the seventeenth century, some new intermediate forms between the pure recitative and the aria. Some of these involved substantial accompaniments containing several obbligato instrumental parts. It is important here to distinguish the *accompanied recitative*, which is still directly subservient to the poetic text, from the *arioso* (q.v.), which is more melodic and has a more regular beat. Both were used frequently in the operas, cantatas, oratorios and *grands motets* of the seventeenth and eighteenth centuries. In these forms they serve as transitions between the pure recitative (the French *recitative simple*, the Italian *recitativo secco*) and the aria.

But whereas the pure recitative disappeared in the nineteenth century (Rossini provides the last examples of *recitativo secco*), the accompanied recitative was to give birth to a new dramatic style: in Wagner recitative, arioso and aria tend to melt together, forming a kind of perpetual melodic line, guided solely by the requirements of the drama. A similar concept made its triumphal appearance at the beginning of the twentieth century, with Debussy's *Pelléas*: here, for the first time, the vocal phrase adapts itself with great suppleness to the shape and rhythm of the words themselves throughout the entire composition. In a quite different spirit Berg, in *Wozzeck*, replaced the recitative with the expressionistic device of the spoken melody (*sprechgesang*).

Although certain composers—like Beethoven in the finale of his Ninth Symphony—have adapted it to instrumental and orchestral styles, the recitative remains essentially a vocal form.

STRUCTURE.

The very principle of the recitative is diametrically opposed to the notion of a definite musical architecture. Its primary concern is to achieve a synthesis between the melodic phrase and the spoken phrase. The Italian language, with its rapid delivery and strong accentuations, lends itself to the voluble *recitativo secco,* the closest thing to the spoken word. Generally accompanied only by the harpsichord, this type of recitative consists in melodic patterns punctuated, at the end of each phrase, by a cadence (Fig. 8).

The French *récitatif simple* is more supple rhythmically, since it often calls for frequent changes of beat (Fig. 9).

Nevertheless considerable metrical freedom characterizes both these forms of pure recitative. The progression of the dramatic action is the objective of both, and they are often in dialogue form. The accompanied, or *obbligato*, recitative,

Fig. 8. *The Marriage of Figaro* (Mozart).

Fig. 9. *Zaïs* (Rameau). Zélidie's recitative.

more meditative and expressive, is almost always presented in monologue form. The *basso continuo* is here replaced by the orchestra (or at least by the strings). The beat is much more regular. At times pure recitative and accompanied recitative alternate in the course of the same section: in the *Passion According to St. Matthew* each time the voice of Christ is heard he is sustained by the violins, whereas the voices of the other characters are supported only by the *basso continuo*. The role of the orchestra is obviously much more important in the modern forms of accompanied recitative; nevertheless in Debussy's *Pelléas* the orchestra almost always remains in the background.

REQUIEM

The *Requiem mass* differs from the ordinary mass not only by its funereal character but also by the order and number of the different parts it comprises. Originally the text of the mass for the dead was confined to Gregorian chant; later it was set to music by a few sixteenth-century polyphonists such as Roland de Lassus and Victoria. But it did not come into its own until the nineteenth century, when Berlioz, Schumann, Liszt, Verdi and Fauré, following the example of Mozart, whose *Requiem* (1791), was his last composition, took the Requiem mass as the point of departure for a kind of enormous cantata or concert mass in which arias and choruses alternate, supported by a very substantial orchestra. This concept is still favored by some composers (Britten, Duruflé).

STRUCTURE.

In the Requiem mass, the *Gloria* and the *Credo* are absent. The mass opens with the *Introit* (*Requiem aeternam dona eis*) and the verse from the psalm *Te decet hymnus*, continues with the *Kyrie*, then with the *Gradual* (*Requiem aeternam*), a brief passage on the *Absolve* and the sequence *Dies irae*; then comes the *Offertory* (*Domine Jesus Christe, sanctus et Benedictus*), the *Agnus Dei* and finally the *Communion* (*Lux aeterna*).

RHAPSODY

The *rhapsody*, a kind of fantasy in a very free style, based on folk songs—or on very simple themes that can serve as an equivalent—is essentially an instrumental form; we might even say that it is fully effective only as an orchestral form. Its affinities with folk music are often very apparent, as in Liszt's *Hungarian Rhapsodies* or Lalo's *Norwegian Rhapsody*, which are among the most famous nineteenth-century compositions in this category. In the twentieth century the undisputed master of this form is Bela Bartok, almost all of whose instrumental compositions, from the quartets to the concerti, although often carefully constructed, partake of the free spirit of the rhapsody. This form may be defined as an uninterrupted succession of contrasting episodes, all relatively short. Understandably a form based on such principle does not lend itself well to any definite structures.

RICERCARE

The *ricercare* (literally "to search") is an instrumental composition of very free structure that imitates the vocal motet. First conceived for the lute, then for the organ or the harpsichord, this form, whose character is more austere than that of the canzone, made its appearance at the beginning of the sixteenth century. The Italians called it *ricercare, fantasia* or *capriccio;* the English called it *fancy;* but the form also existed in Spain, Germany and France. In the seventeenth century the ricercare became a set form; under the impetus of Titelouze, Sweelinck, Frescobaldi and Froberger it evolved in the direction of the fugue, to which it ultimately gave birth. By the eighteenth century the word *ricercare* was hardly ever used, except to designate, paradoxically, a sort of specially constructed fugue. (See *Canzone; Fantasy; Fugue.*)

STRUCTURE.

Like the motet, from which it derives, the ricercare uses imitative contrapuntal writing. It is usually made up of several episodes (anywhere from three to nine), each of which brings into play a different motif. The tempo and key are the only sources of unity. This arbitrary juxtaposition of several themes was justifiable in the motet, since the configuration was determined by the words; here it is less so. However, certain monothematic ricercares by the Gabrielis, and those of Frescobaldi and Froberger, even more thoroughly constructed, were already closely akin to the eighteenth-century fugue.

ROMANCE

The *romance* is a love song, particularly sentimental, dating from the pre-romantic and romantic era. It differs from the ballad, its contemporary, by the absence of

any dramatic or tragic component, and on a musical plane
by the absolute preponderance of the melody. As a vocal
composition it is a sort of lied, aristocratic rather than popular; it possesses the facileness and the superficial refinement
of drawing room music. It preserves these characteristics as
an instrumental composition, although occasionally developing along broader lines (the slow movement of Schumann's
Fourth Symphony).

In France the vocal romance with piano, harp or guitar
accompaniment was once very popular. Minor composers
like Gossec, Grètry and Boïeldieu cultivated this form,
which, in more ways than one, was an outgrowth of the old
air de cour (q.v.) and was soon to be supplanted by the *mélodie*, an infinitely richer form.

STRUCTURE.

Generally the romance has no well-defined structure. It
often borrows that of the rondo or the lied form. However,
the French romance is nearly always in stanza form, made
up of verses and ritornellos, to which was sometimes added
an ornamental recitative by way of introduction. From the
seventeenth-century air de cour it borrowed the partly improvised *double*, in which the singer showed off his or her
voice by inventing variants, which probably gave rise to re-
grettable self-indulgences.

RONDO

The *rondo*—which the French used to spell *rondeau*, like the medieval vocal form from which it seems to have grown (although there is no proof of this)—is an instrumental form that was extremely widespread in the seventeenth and eighteenth centuries. Scarcely a suite from the French school fails to include one or more rondos. The harpsichord works of François Couperin, among others, are primarily built around this form. It was retained in the classical sonata and symphony alike. "Rondo" had then become synonymous with "brilliant piece, to be played in a lively fashion": it was assigned the role of finale formerly reserved for the gigue. After a momentary eclipse toward the end of the nineteenth century the rondo has made fleeting reappearances in the works of contemporary masters (the *Sacrificial Dance* in Stravinsky's *Rite of Spring;* the *Dance Steps* in Schoenberg's *Septet*).

STRUCTURE.

The rondo is characterized by the alternation of the principal phrase—the subject—with a series of different secondary episodes. If the subject is represented by A, we get the pattern ABACADA and so on. The subject is fairly short: it generally comprises eight to sixteen measures. Among the French masters of the seventeenth and eighteenth centuries the episodes are generally of the same length. Sometimes they contain elements taken from the subject (Rameau's *La Joyeuse*); sometimes they derive from it more or less di-

rectly (*Les Niais de Sologne*); however, they may also differ
from it completely. They are written either in the main key,
like the subject, or in a closely related key. There may be
any number of them.

The sonata-rondo. The classical composers further developed the rondo when they adopted it as the finale of their
sonatas and symphonies. The episodes became much longer
than the subject, which may be re-exposed in different keys.
Often the first episode shifts into the dominant key and involves a kind of second theme that appears again in the last
episode in the original key; the middle episode, which brings
in new elements, acts as a modulating development (finale of
Mozart's Sonata in B flat), whence an obvious analogy with
the sonata form.

SCHERZO

The *scherzo* is a composition in two parts whose
construction is reminiscent of the minuet's. Like the minuet,
it is in triple time, but the tempo is much quicker. It made its
appearance at the beginning of the nineteenth century. True,
the Italians used the term *scherzo* (meaning "banter, ca-
price") to designate jovial compositions, either secular
melodies or instrumental pieces. However, the scherzo did
not become a musical form in the full sense until Beethoven;
he was the first to organize it and assign it a role in the
sonata and symphony, as a replacement for the minuet. It
differed from the latter in that it was more modern (no
longer dancelike), and in its rhythm. Chopin treated the
scherzo as an independent composition. In both these forms
it was much in favor throughout the nineteenth century; nor

has it been neglected in the twentieth (a noteworthy example is contained in Berg's *Lyric Suite*).

STRUCTURE.

Like the minuet, from which it developed, the scherzo comprises two distinct sections. The first is called *scherzo,* the second *trio.* They offer a thematic contrast accentuated by the fact they are written in different keys. Each section is divided in turn into three periods, the first suspensive, the second modulating and the third conclusive; this third period constitutes a re-exposition of the first, in accordance with the ABA' pattern. And indeed the overall structure of the piece follows the ABA pattern, since the first of the two sections is repeated as a *da capo* at the end of the trio, another feature common to both the scherzo and the minuet. However, Beethoven, applying a century in advance the advice of Schoenberg (". . . never write anything your copyist could write for you") contrived to vary this repetition of the first piece by introducing certain changes and by adding a coda. Schumann gave even more variety to the form by adding a second trio, which gives us the pattern ABACA.

However, the essential difference from the minuet is that the central period (B) is almost always handled as a modulating development, conceived in the spirit of the central development of the sonata allegro.

SERENADE

The *serenade* was orginally for voice, but it ultimately became almost exclusively instrumental. It stands midway between the divertimento and the symphony: while more fully developed and technically more sophisticated than the divertimento, it does not have the dimensions of the symphony nor does it usually demand as large an orchestra; moreover its style is more "lilting." The serenade was much in vogue during the "drawing room" period (second half of the eighteenth century). Mozart in particular, then in the service of the Archbishop of Salzburg, wrote a number of them for either the dinner table or open-air performance.

The moderns (Roussel, Schoenberg, Stravinsky, Milhaud) have again taken up this form, which had fallen somewhat into disuse during the nineteenth century. (See *Cassation; Divertimento.*)

STRUCTURE.

The structure of the serenade resembles that of the old suite—by its many movements—and the symphony—by its construction. It often consists of five or six pieces, sometimes even more: Mozart's *Haffner Serenade* (K. 250) has no less than eight; his *Serenata Notturna* (K. 239), on the other hand, consists of only a march, a minuet and a rondo.

SINFONIA

The *sinfonia* is a very ill-defined form, or to be more exact, a form that has had many successive definitions. At the beginning of the seventeenth century the sinfonia was an instrumental, homo-rhythmic composition, as distinguished from the *sonata* or *canzone da sonar*, which were essentially polyphonic. Toward the middle of the century, however, a new distinction appeared: the sinfonia became a sonata placed at the beginning of a partita or a lyric composition. Starting with Lully, the terms *sinfonia* and *ouverture à l'italienne* became synonymous. Then, by extension, it became customary to apply the word *sinfonia* to any orchestral composition in one or several movements. This eventually led to the classical *symphony* about the middle of the eighteenth century, a form much richer in style, and more balanced in structure. The sinfonia still survived for some years in the form of the Italian overture, but disappeared before the end of the eighteenth century. (See *Canzone; Overture; Sonata.*)

SINFONIA CONCERTANTE

The *sinfonia concertante* constitutes a synthesis of the symphony with the old *concerto grosso*: it is a kind of concerto for several soloists (usually two or three), the style and structure of which are those of the symphony. This form was very popular during the last third of the eighteenth century (Mozart wrote in this field), but its more recent history has not been very outstanding: the nineteenth century ignored it almost completely—unless Brahms' *Double Concerto* for violin and cello, for example, comes under this heading. In the twentieth century we might cite the *Sinfonia Concertante* of Frank Martin.

SONATA

The *sonata* is an instrumental composition in several movements, ordinarily very highly developed, and designed for a small number of performers, usually one or two. Therefore it seems reasonable to place it under the heading of chamber music, for it possesses the technical potential and expressive power we associate with that genre. We might be tempted to demonstrate that the sonata is basically a "concerted" form* except that ever since Kuhnau there has existed a type of sonata for solo instrument that certainly cannot be considered an inferior form, even though some composers have made it a vehicle for superficial and completely digital virtuosity. Nevertheless in support of such a thesis, we could argue that insofar as the sonata for solo instrument was most often conceived for the keyboard it retained certain polyphonic possibilities, which Beethoven, for example—although the inventor of a purely "dynamic" type of sonata—exploited in full.

The sonata, which appeared in Italy at the beginning of the seventeenth century, was a result of the fusion of the *canzone* with the *suite* (q.v.), a fusion that was for many years nothing but a *confusion*. Toward the end of the sixteenth century, we know, the Italians gave the name *canzone da sonar* to any piece destined to be played ("sounded") on instruments (organ, brass or strings). Only later was the term *sonata* introduced to designate an instrumental composition of polyphonic character, as opposed to the *sinfonia*,

---

* Originally it was: later we shall see that the seventeenth century was the period of the *trio-sonata*.

written in a more homo-rhythmic style. At the beginning of
the seventeenth century the sonata was a minor form; it
usually served as an introduction or an interlude in a vocal
composition, either cantata or opera. About 1650 the Germans began to place sonatas at the beginning of their suites
or partitas. A little later they often gave the title *sonata* to
suites in several movements that contained no reference to
dance music. During that same period (ca. 1670) the Italians distinguished between the church sonata (*sonatta da
chiesa*), fuguelike in style, and the suite of dances, which
they entitled chamber sonata (*sonatta da camera*). However, the two forms still had a number of points in common:
the church sonata and the chamber sonata alike generally
comprised four movements, alternately slow and fast, both
dominated by the violin; it was customary to write these
pieces for violin and *basso continuo*, or, more frequently, for
two violins and *basso continuo* (trio-sonata). At the end of
the seventeenth century Couperin introduced the Italian
sonata into France. A little later the Germans broadened the
form: Kuhnau adapted it to the solo harpsichord, while J. S.
Bach wrote the first sonatas for violin and harpsichord
obbligato. Then, about the middle of the eighteenth century,
occurred the great development that ultimately produced the
classical sonata. Henceforth all kinship with the suite, already on the wane in any case, was completely excluded.
With Karl Philipp Emanuel Bach, Boccherini and Stamitz,
the ternary and bithematic structure of the sonata became
crystallized, while at the same time the notion of *development* appeared, acquiring all its meaning in the works of
Haydn, Mozart and Beethoven. The sonata form was born.
From the end of the eighteenth century on it was to become
the archetypal structure of chamber music and even of
symphonic music. Since Debussy many composers have
sought to get away from it, while others keep returning to it
periodically.

STRUCTURE.

In his authoritative *Cours de Composition Musicale*, to which this book owes a great debt, Vincent d' Indy sets forth the three essential differences he sees between the sonata and the suite:

1. The reduction of the number of movements to three or four (sometimes five).
2. The substitution of the *style galant* for the polyphonic fuguelike style.
3. The gradual appearance of the ternary arrangement, at first monothematic, then bithematic.

Vincent d'Indy lays great stress on this last, which he regards as essential. Thus he does not hesitate to trace the origins of the sonata to Corelli, whom he claims to have been the first to establish the concept of returning to the original melodic design in the main key.

Without trying to belittle the significance of this innovation—which, by introducing the idea of re-exposition, prepared the way for the ternary arrangement of the future classical sonata—there is reason to believe that d'Indy is stressing a problem of structure that does not concern the real *essence* of the form. Nor is this essence affected by the number of movements: in fact many suites written in Corelli's time had only four parts. As for the substitution of the *style galant* for the polyphonic style, it marked the passing of an era, the word *style* being understood here in its most intimate relationship with a given form. In any case this substitution did not take place in Corelli's time, but much later.

On the other hand, Vincent d'Indy may perhaps underestimate the fact that the Italian and German masters of the seventeenth century and the beginning of the eighteenth gradually acquired the habit of replacing the dance titles of their chamber sonata movements with simple indications of tempo. It was not purely a matter of chance that the allemande became *allegro*, the saraband *adagio* and the gigue *presto*; these new names correspond to a firm determination to divest these pieces completely of their dancelike character. If the definitions at the beginning of this book are correct, such a modification had a more direct effect on the spirit of the form, and thus on the form itself, than the considerations of structure and period style stressed in d'Indy's *Cours de Composition*.

The problems of structure raised by the sonata remain nonetheless extremely important: more so, perhaps, than those in any other form. This is because the development of the sonata represents one of the most remarkable attempts of the human mind to organize a world of sound that, by its many-faceted dimensions, transcends even the most complex monothematic structures. For this reason the different structures successively adopted by the sonata and, through it, symphonic and chamber music should be reviewed with particular care. For although the sonata certainly cannot be defined by its structure alone, it is impossible to define it without taking its structure into account.

The pre-classical sonata. The seventeenth century was the period of the *sonate à trois*, or trio-sonata, for two violins and *basso continuo* (viola da gamba) or cello, doubled or not by a harmonizing instrument—harpsichord, organ or lute—whose function was to "actualize the figuring." This type of sonata was essentially polyphonic, whereas the sonata for one violin and *basso continuo*, which did not come to the fore until the beginning of the eighteenth century, obviously leaned toward a more monodic idiom. The work of Corelli (end of the seventeenth century) epitomizes fairly well the tendencies of this pre-classical period, in which for the most part sonatas and suites are hardly distinguishable structurally. Indeed the structure of the sonata, far from being fixed, was then in an experimental stage; in all his works Corelli was seeking to achieve a balance, constantly trying new devices. Although most of his chamber sonata movements follow the traditional practice of borrowing the "binary form" of the *suite* (q.v.), others follow the ternary construction ABA, with the first exposition of A usually ending on the relative, which leads to the need for a change of key when it comes time for the re-exposition. The *graves* and the fuguelike movements of his church sonatas are handled with great freedom: indeed frequently the initial design of a *grave* is neither repeated nor even referred to in the rest of the section. At times—although this does not mean we are dealing with a second theme—the principal design of an allegro is divided into two fragments, the first in the tonic, the second in the dominant (gigue from sonata No. 4, Opus 4). Did Corelli have an even more direct premonition of the classical sonata and its contrasts when he interpolated several short adagio sections into an allegro movement (Opus 3, No. 12)? Did he have an intuitive grasp of what would one day be the cyclical form (so dear to the heart of César Franck), when he established relationships between the themes of the different movements (Opus 1, No. 10; Opus 2, Nos. 1 and 3; Opus 5, No. 10)? Corelli was a composer of genius, but not to that degree! Besides, none of these constructions belonged to him alone; many other composers had employed them before him. The fact remains, however, that Corelli's works constitute a kind of clearing house for all his contemporaries' efforts.

Vincent d'Indy, as we have seen, held that it was Corelli who "discovered" the re-exposition of the initial design in the principal key. Whether the master of Fusignano invented the resulting ternary structure is of little importance. It is more interesting to follow the process that led to this discovery. Does not the ternary arrangement appear, after all, to be a sort of compromise between the *aria da capo* and the "binary form" of the suite? Setting aside the changes of detail that occur in the re-exposition, the gavotte that constitutes the finale of the sonata No. 2, Opus 2, would be a perfect example of the *da capo* if the A part did not end in the dominant, as it would in a binary section. How does the allegro of the sonata No. 11, Opus 5, whose two repeats end on the tonic, differ from the *da capo* form, except for the fact that A' in this case is not a simple repetition of A, but differs from it to the same extent to which the second part of a binary piece sometimes differs from the first?

In general, these structural considerations concern only the main section of the sonata, that is, mostly the first allegro, which during the eighteenth century became the opening piece as well, as the Corelli-type prelude gradually shrank to a short—and optional—introduction. We may concur with Vincent d'Indy when he says that "the main effort of the symphonic composer seems always to have been concentrated on this same first section, the only one that, by a strange hiatus in the vocabulary of music, has never had a name of its own." * However, this preponderance of the first allegro of the "sonata form"—as it is usually called, for want of a better name—must not make us lose sight of the composition as a whole.

In Corelli's time the sonata usually comprised four movements, ordinarily arranged according to the pattern S.F.S.F.† A few church sonatas and a larger number of chamber sonatas included five movements and more; but certain slow movements were only transitional episodes, amounting to but a few measures.

The classical sonata form. Superficially the pre-classical sonata and the classical sonata seem to obey two entirely different musical systems. However, a closer examination of the evolution of the form shows that the transition from one to the other took place almost imperceptibly. The introduction of a single novel feature—the re-entry of the theme in the opening key—was enough to differentiate the ternary

* V. d'Indy, *Cours de Composition*, II, 1, p. 158.
† S: slow movement; F: fast movement.

pattern of the sonata allegro from the binary pattern of the
suite. Once this arrangement was generally adopted by the
eighteenth-century masters they naturally turned their attention to the internal organization of each of the three parts.
We have seen that in the pre-classical sonata the first section
tended to move toward the dominant or the relative, and that
this new key was frequently stated by the intermediary
agency of a secondary pattern, B, generally derived from A,
which remained the only theme. The history of the sonata in
the eighteenth century is the history of the emancipation of
B. Little by little it freed itself from A—ceased to imitate it,
and acquired characteristics of its own, which later were
carried to the point of systematic contrast. As firmly en-
trenched in the dominant or the relative as A can be in the
tonic, B asserted its right to equality; the second theme had
come into existence. This resulted in the subdivision of the
first part or exposition into two distinct sections (even three,
if we count the transition necessary to bind the sections):
the tonic section, devoted entirely to A, and the "dominant"
section, centered on B. In the third part (re-exposition) the
problem is different: the need to end in the main key makes
it necessary to transpose section B from the dominant key
into the tonic. Between these two parts lies the middle part,
to which the composer turns his attention only after the
exposition and re-exposition have been definitely organized.

Although the Beethoven sonata, in which this middle section acquired real scope and significance, was still a thing of
the future, still as early as the mid-eighteenth century it de-
served the name *development* that we give it today. Little by
little it ceased to be a simple play of modulations amounting
to the repetition of a single design; soon it became a genuine
thematic process in which the themes were analyzed and
broken down into their component parts.

Rather than by analyzing a score, we feel, the reader can
obtain the clearest notion of the way this form developed

from the time of Corelli to that of K.P.E. Bach and Haydn by examining a chart in which the usual plan of the opening allegro of the classical sonata is compared with the corresponding piece in a pre-classical composition. It is important to remember, however, that this is merely an outline, with all the rigidity that implies; in practice, many a sonata's allegro movement deviates more or less from the pattern, either because theme B is repeated in the re-exposition before theme A (Mozart's Sonata in C minor, K. 457) or because the development takes for its theme the motif of the final cadence in the first part (Sonata in C major, K. 545), or a new element is introduced (Sonata in G major, K. 283), or the re-entry of A occurs in the subdominant (Sonata in C major, K. 545). Sometimes the principal part is constructed on an entirely different arrangement from that of the "sonata form"; this occurs in the Sonata in A major (K. 331), in which the first movement is a theme and variations. The same holds for the pre-classical sonata. The following chart must therefore be regarded only as a guide.

The Allegro of the Sonata

Pre-Classical Monothematic	Classical (Sonata Form) Bithematic
I. Exposition	I. Exposition
1. Theme A, in the main key.	1. Theme A, in the main key.
2. B, derived from A, moves toward the dominant. Normally the exposition ends in the dominant.	2. Modulating transition, called *bridge* (toward the dominant).
	3. Theme B, in the dominant; this theme, which at times still derives from A,

normally comprises **three** phrases: b′ b″ b‴.

4. Cadence ending in the dominant (at times the motif of this cadence is so prominent that it may be regarded as a third theme (C).

II. Divertimento
Modulating part: imitations on A or B, preparing for the return to the main key.

II. Development
Modulating thematic operations involving A, B, sometimes C, if warranted, preparing for the return to the main key.

III. Re-Exposition
1. Theme A, in the main key.
2. B, also in the main key.

III. Re-Exposition
1. Theme A, in the main key.
2. Bridge, leading this time to the main key.
3. Theme B, in the main key.
4. Cadence, ending in the main key.

About the middle of the eighteenth century the sonata generally included only three movements, less often four, occasionally two. Although they were certainly not as richly constructed as the main movements, the others were in the process of being organized as well. The problem was to endow each with its specific structure, thus eliminating the last vestiges of the suite. The slow movement took its cue from the opening allegro, which it followed, and adopted another ternary-type construction,* the lied form. (See *Lied.*) It became an established custom to compose it in a key closely related to the main key. The *minuet* (q.v.),

* Mozart often gave it the same structure as the opening allegro.

which was optional, tended to follow the sonata form. The finale borrowed the rondo form (q.v.) from the French school. Before long the rondo evolved in a richer direction, toward the sonata-rondo.

The Beethoven sonata. Beethoven did not abandon the framework of the sonata form developed by his predecessors. However, he incorporated into it such bold, new conceptions that he may be regarded as the creator of a new type of sonata. With Beethoven the theme is no longer a simple design; it becomes, so to speak, an idea, a character. This explains the sharp difference between the two main themes in the allegro movement of a Beethoven sonata: A is the masculine principle, B the feminine principle, and they behave accordingly. Although in the non-modulating parts they are merely "depicted," the modulating passages—i.e., the transitions and developments—become a kind of drama, with each theme playing the dominant role in turn. The importance of the development in the Beethoven sonata is therefore relatively much greater than in the eighteenth-century sonata. Moreover the Beethoven development brings to bear certain ideas that, though not all absolutely new, had never before been organized to such an extent. Vincent d'Indy distinguishes six different types of development in Beethoven's sonatas (and symphonies):

1. *Rhythmic development:* the repetition of a rhythm already heard, but in combination with another melody and other harmonies.

2. *Melodic development:* the melody remains intact, while the rhythm and the harmony change.

3. *Harmonic development:* the harmony remains the same, while the rhythm and the melody are altered.

4. *Amplification:* by adding supplementary notes or enlarging the scope of the melody, a particular thematic element is given special emphasis.

5. *Elimination:* the inverse process, consisting in suppressing certain essential notes of the theme.

6. *Superposition:* several themes or fragments of themes are heard simultaneously.

Another peculiarity of the Beethoven sonata is that the division of B into three phrases, already hinted at in the classical sonata, becomes a rule. Also worth noting is the more extensive development of the "bridge" between A and B, in both the exposition and the re-exposition, and the increasingly frequent use of a final coda following the re-exposition; this coda, sometimes quite long, is often preceded by a second development.

Setting aside certain unusual compositions (Opus 111 for instance), the general pattern of the Beethoven sonata differs little from the traditional pattern. Most of Beethoven's sonatas are in three movements; a few involve only two. As for the four-movement sonatas, we have already seen how Beethoven replaced the minuet with a *scherzo* (q.v.), usually interpolated between the slow movement and the finale. As in the classical sonata, the slow movement uses the lied form as enlarged by Beethoven (developed lied, sonata-lied), and the finale of the rondo—or, more accurately, the sonata-rondo (see these terms).

The idea of the need for a formal identity between the various movements, abandoned with the disappearance of the suite, was reappearing. The three essential parts of the sonata were tending toward a similar structure, since the sonata-lied and the sonata-rondo obviously stemmed from the sonata form. However, this was not the only way the idea of unity was making progress. Returning, consciously or otherwise, to a concept dear to the German and Italian masters of the seventeenth century, Beethoven conceived the idea of building an entire sonata or symphony on a single theme; better still, on a single cell. This was to be the origin of the cyclical sonata, ultimately perfected by César Franck, in the wake of the experiments by Schumann and Liszt.

The cyclical sonata. The cell is the most characteristic of the patterns of sound that make up a theme and consequently the one the composer uses most often in constructing his compositions. By definition it is irreducible; it cannot be simplified, it cannot be deprived of a single note, without losing all significance.

The cell may be rhythmic (Fig. 10) or melodic (Fig. 11).

Fig. 10. *Sonata,* Opus 106 (Beethoven).
Fig. 11. *Violin Sonata* (Franck).

Fig. 12. *Sonata* (Franck).

The often-cited example of Franck's *Violin Sonata* is typical of the use of the generative cell: this simple figure is indeed at the root of the principal themes around which the four movements of this work are organized. Some authorities see two other secondary cells (Fig. 12), but both obviously grow from the mother cell, the characteristic element of which is not so much the interval of a third or the number of the notes as it is the ascending motion that leads to a broad expressive accent followed by a descending motion. In this view the so-called secondary cells are simply variants of the original cell: they display the same ascending and descending motion (expressed twice in the second) and the same accent on the uppermost note in the melodic pattern.

Of course every theme contains a cell: we could easily find the cell of the subject of a seventeenth-century fugue. As we have seen, however, the idea of development through the analysis and subdivision of themes did not appear until the following century. This is why it was not until the nineteenth century that it occurred to anyone that the entire cycle of a sonata or a symphony might be built wholly from a single subdivision of a theme.*

In Franck's time other, similar tendencies appeared. Liszt had already tried to recast the sonata in a spirit akin to the cyclical concept; but his B minor Piano Sonata, written more than twenty years before the major works of the Franco-Belgian master, suffers less from the very free construction that relates it to the fantasy than from an obvious weakness in its thematic development. Brahms and Fauré seemed to preserve the classical mold; but the former used the cyclical device on several occasions (*Sonata for Violin and Piano*, Opus 78), while the latter used a profusion of unexpected modulations. However, all these sonatas have some features in common: the abundance of their modulations, the boldness of their tonal structure, their harmonic richness, a fondness for dissonance, and, in some cases (Franck, for instance), an ever-increasing chromaticism, which shows that Wagner's influence even included chamber music. The breakdown of the tonal system was just around the corner. It came with the appearance of Arnold Schoenberg.

Schoenberg's sonata-suite. While the French school of the early twentieth century was temporarily giving the style, but not the structure, of the sonata a new lease on life (if only by trying to simplify it), Schoenberg was discovering a new world of sound: the world of atonality. Having explored it, he undertook to organize it, and to achieve this goal he forged a tool: the twelve-tone row. Here the ideal theme

---

* It is only fair to point out that semi-cyclical compositions such as the *Art of the Fugue* had already achieved this unity, although entirely differently.

takes the form of a row of twelve notes including all twelve tones of the chromatic scale. Presented at first in their original order, these twelve notes may be inverted or reversed or both; with each repetition their rhythm may be altered. Thus a sort of perpetual variation is created, which seems indeed one of the most fascinating aspects of Schoenberg's universe. Rightly or wrongly, the Viennese master contrived to fit this concept of his into the mold of the sonata form (Overture from his *Suite,* Opus 29). In Schoenberg's compositions this structure preserves some of its Beethoven-like features: when he deliberately avoids any literal repetitions of fragments of the exposition in writing his re-exposition, is he not carrying to its conclusion the spirit of constant renewal we find in the last sonatas of the master of Bonn?

The reader may be surprised to find the term *sonata form* used in connection with a composition entitled *Suite*. This contradiction is only apparent. Actually Schoenberg created in this composition a new type of sonata, which might be called *sonata-suite*, by borrowing some of the special structural features of the first and the overall structure of the second. Often a single theme derived from the work's generative row supplies the material for the various movements, thereby rejoining the cyclical tradition. In one of the most famous row compositions of this type, Alban Berg's *Lyric Suite* for string quartet,* each of the six parts grows from one or more motifs or themes already heard in a preceding movement. The first movement is the only—and obvious—exception; but this does not make it the least interesting, quite the contrary. It consists of an exposition and a re-exposition, without any central development; however, a closer examination of the score shows that the development is included in both the exposition and re-exposition, in the form of a perpetual variation. This composition contains

* I ask the reader to excuse my having had to borrow these examples from compositions that certainly cannot be regarded as sonatas. We must not forget that the sonata is the basis of all chamber music.

several structures peculiar to the sonata, notably the rondo (second movement) and the scherzo (third and fifth movements). As for the cell idea, there is no clearer example of it than the *Quartet*, Opus 28 of Anton Webern, another of Schoenberg's disciples. For obviously in this work the entire row—and consequently the composition as a whole—derives from the four notes that spell out the name BACH. (Fig. 13).

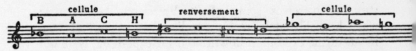

Fig. 13. *Quartet*, Opus 28 (Webern). This "row" is constructed entirely on the four notes that, in the German system of notation, spell out the name BACH.

Thus summarized—too briefly, no doubt—the evolution of the sonata structure and the forms derived from it is seen to be a logical sequence of new acquisitions, a ceaseless search for unity through ever-increasing diversity. As soon as the artist achieves a balance, he is forced to destroy it by the introduction of a new element. The suite, in its binary uniformity, was a perfectly balanced form. The appearance of the second theme and the disparity of the various movements raised a problem that the whole history of the sonata has constituted an attempt to solve. This perpetual process of calling in question has resulted in increasingly complex musical structures, which may tend to confuse the listener, already disturbed by so much dissonance; often he feels he is dealing with a radical departure from past forms when he is merely faced with an extension of them.

SUITE

The *suite* is a succession (as the French word implies) of dance movements different in character but identical in key and, usually, in structure. Of all the composite instrumental forms (that is, involving several movements) it is the oldest: its origin is in the Middle Ages, when it was already customary to couple certain dances. In the sixteenth century the Italian lutists often linked two pairs of dances, sometimes adding a postlude in the form of a toccata. The *double* (or variation) also appeared at that time. The style of the suite blossomed during the seventeenth century, under the impetus of composers in Italy (from Frescobaldi to Corelli), Germany (Peurl, Froberger, Schein) and England (Locke, Purcell), who endowed it with great polyphonic richness. At the end of the seventeenth century the *Ordres* of François Couperin were among the outstanding compositions in this genre. In the eighteenth century Bach's famous *Partitas* (or *German Suites*) constituted a final stage of development beyond which no further progress was possible. Under the influence of the *style galant*, which came into vogue in the second half of the eighteenth century, the suite was replaced by the *divertimento*, the *serenade* and the *cassation* (q.v.), which constituted departures from it in both structure and musical idiom. A few efforts to bring back the suite have been made in the twentieth century. Ravel, Milhaud and Schoenberg in particular have sought to revive this form that has lain neglected so long.

STRUCTURE.

The archetypal structure of the suite, as introduced by
Froberger in 1650, is based on a succession of slow or
moderately slow movements and fast movements. It comprises at least four parts: allemande, courante, saraband and
gigue. Between the saraband and the gigue, however, other
dances could be interpolated: for example, a pair of minuets
(Bach's First French Suite) or a gavotte and an aria (Fourth
French Suite). Sometimes quite a few of these optional
pieces appear: the Sixth French Suite contains four, which
brings the total of movements to eight.

Among the other dances most frequently incorporated in
the suite—or in the Italian chamber sonata, built along similar lines—were the pavan, the gaillarde, the bourrée, the
rigaudon, the loure, the forlane, the saltarella, the branle, the
passepied, the chaconne and the passacaglia. Because of
their length the chaconne and the passacaglia almost always
have the concluding role (Partita in D minor for solo violin,
by J. S. Bach). The saraband is occasionally replaced by an
aria. Finally, frequent use is made of the double, which we
shall define in a moment.

The allemande, the opening section of the suite, is often
preceded by a long prelude (J. S. Bach's *German Suites*).
When this prelude takes the form of an overture in the
French style, the order of the various sections that follow is
generally changed. Here we deal with what we might regard
as a different type of suite, as evinced by the title *overtures*
that J. S. Bach applied to his orchestral suites, all of which
are conceived in this way. The First Suite in C major comprises an overture in the strict sense, a courante, a double
gavotte, a forlane, a double minuet, a double bourrée and a
double passepied (each of the double pieces being repeated
da capo).

The partita. Partita was the name the Germans gave the

suite. However, a shade of meaning here should be stressed. The term *partita* usually implies variation (Bach called his chorales with variations *partitas*). Indeed, in the German tradition the other movements of the suite often grew directly from the first movement. This interdependence, which is not particularly strict, comes from the use of common motifs and a similarity of modulations. Although many suites entitled *partita* do not follow this rule, the majority do. The Italian *chamber sonata* often observes it as well (Sonata No. 2, by Vitali).

The ordre. Certain French masters—François Couperin and his disciples—entitled their suites *ordres*. If the suite is held to have a well-established structure—the structure fixed by Froberger—the ordre is not always a suite; but we have seen that the suites of French origin, or at any rate all those that fall under the heading of the French overture, also depart from the Froberger model. We may therefore regard the ordre as a suite with a free overall structure, often comprising a large number of pieces.

Les Folies Françaises, by Couperin, consists of a dozen pieces with charmingly suggestive titles:

1. Virginity (in an invisible domino).
2. Modesty (in a pink domino).
3. Ardor (in a flesh-colored domino).
4. Hope (in a green domino).
5. Fidelity (in a blue domino).
6. Perseverance (in a flax-gray domino).
7. Languor (in a violet domino).
8. Coquetry (in various dominoes).
9. The Old Beaux and the Out-of-Date Paymistresses (in purple dominoes and in dominoes the color of dead leaves).
10. Voluntary Assistance (in a yellow domino).
11. Sullen Jealousy (in a domino of Moorish gray).
12. Frenzy or Despair (in a black domino).

The modern suite. The contemporary suite is often even freer in arrangement. Concerned as they are with reviving the old forms, some composers have written suites comprising fugues, a form that in the seventeenth and eighteenth centuries played only a very exceptional and episodic role within the framework of the introductory piece (prelude or overture). Ravel's *Tombeau de Couperin* is in six parts: prelude, fugue, forlane, rigaudon, minuet and toccata. Milhaud's Second Symphonic Suite includes an overture, a prelude and fugue, a pastorale, a nocturne and a finale. Schoenberg's sonata-suites have an even more complex structure, undeniably bound up with the *sonata* (q.v.).

Internal structure: the "binary form." If we except the pieces treated in rondo form (very frequent in the French *ordres*, but much rarer among German and Italian composers), and those in which the spirit of the variation is predominant (the chaconne and the passacaglia), all the movements of the suite cleave to the same structure. Just as the ternary arrangement is associated with the sonata, the "binary form"—which the Germans call "two-part lied"—is associated with the suite. But whereas in the classical sonata only the opening movement is traditionally in the sonata form, in the suite the allemande, courante, saraband and gigue (as well as most of the optional movements) are constructed along identical lines. The result is a homogeneity of structure that, together with the use of a single key throughout and—at times—the cyclical utilization of the same motifs, endows the suite with an undeniable unity.

The binary structure divides a movement into two parts of about equal length: about the middle of the piece is a double bar indicating that each of the two parts must be played twice. The first half comes to an end on a cadence in the key of the dominant. If we take as an example a particularly simple piece like the Courante in Bach's Sixth French Suite, we can easily observe how the melody and the harmony, once the opening motif has been exposed, move toward this

new key (fifth measure), modulate into it (eighth measure),
become settled in it (ninth measure), and temporarily con-
clude in it (sixteenth measure). After the double bar the
same operation takes place in reverse; however, this return
to the opening key involves a few incursions along the way
into various closely related keys, giving rise to rapid explora-
tions of the regions of the relative (eighteenth measure), the
second degree (twenty-first measure) and the subdominant
(twenty-sixth measure). The thematic material of this second part is usually borrowed from the first: it contains the
same melodic designs, treated differently. The concluding
figure is always repeated, and the opening motif generally
is.

Sometimes the first part does not end on the dominant,
but on the relative. This key structure especially prevails in
the suites in a minor key: three of the six pieces that make
up the Second French Suite have their central cadence in
the relative. In the eighteenth century this practice became
increasingly prevalent in compositions written in a minor
key; in the classical sonata it was to become a general
rule.

The pattern of the "binary form" (AB) may be summarized as follows:

A. First Part	B. Second Part
Moves from the opening key toward the dominant key or the relative.	Returns through various modulations to the main key.

Doubles. In the course of a suite a given piece is often
followed by its *double*, a sort of ornamental variation.* The
double's origin is very remote: at the end of the fifteenth
century the Spanish *vihuelistas* embellished their dance tunes

---

* Certain pieces include several. This multiplication of the *doubles* is
probably at the origin of the theme and variations of which the classical
composers were so fond.

with improvised *diferencias*. The practice of writing out *doubles* became current in the seventeenth century. Extremely simple in form, these *doubles* amounted to a second statement of the melody in a more or less ornamented form. Thus Bach, following the example of the French masters, designates the *double* of one of the pieces in his Second English Suite as "the ornamentation of the same saraband." However, the *double* could also take the more subtle form of a paraphrase and, though constantly referring to the piece from which it derived, avoid reproducing its exact outlines. The Courante in Bach's Partita in B minor for solo violin has nothing in common with its *double* except the harmony (which is not actually expressed but strongly suggested); however, this bond is sufficient for the ear to link one to the other. (See *Variation*.)

SYMPHONIC POEM

The *symphonic poem* (or tone poem) sums up the essence of "program music." The composer strives to paint and even to narrate; often, however, he does not completely abandon all notion of musical pattern or musical architecture. The symphonic poem is a tableau or drama expressed solely through instruments. As its name indicates, it is usually conceived for a large orchestra, all of whose resources seem required to pursue such an ambitious goal; nevertheless some remarkable symphonic poems have been written for piano alone (*Pictures at an Exhibition*, by Mussorgsky). Before the appearance of the symphonic poem in the nineteenth century many attempts at descriptive music had been made, as far back as the sixteenth century (*Le*

Chant des Oiseaux, by Janequin). However, the symphonic poem does not confine itself to simple description; it is organized around a definite subject, strives to suggest with some degree of precision the various key moments and vicissitudes of some poem or story. In this sense Johann Kuhnau may be regarded as the true precursor of this form. Some compositions called *symphonies* are really symphonic poems (*Symphonie fantastique*, by Berlioz).

STRUCTURE.

The symphonic poem follows the story that inspires it, and has no fixed structure; it may borrow that of any other form, or it may have none whatsoever. Kuhnua's *Biblical Sonatas* for harpsichord, which are considered to be among the oldest known efforts at musical narration, call on all the most common structures of the composer's day (end of the seventeenth century), even when he was describing the most minutely realistic details. In the symphonic poem proper each theme customarily represents a setting or character: each aspect of the story of Strauss' *Till Eulenspiegel* corresponds to a melodic design periodically repeated, so that the composition becomes a kind of rondo. Thus in this case the theme takes on an anecdotal rather than a musical significance. Also, the composer tries to follow his program, so to speak, measure for measure. The case of Debussy's *La Mer* is different, in that every narrative element seems excluded from this purely impressionistic composition, in which the intention—conceived after the fact, perhaps—was to suggest to the listener three aspects of the ocean.

SYMPHONY

The *symphony* is generally a large-scale composition comprising several movements and written for full symphony orchestra, or at least part of an orchestra (*symphony for strings, chamber symphony*). It must be distinguished from the *sinfonia* (q.v.), which was only one of its origins, for chamber music had at least as much influence on its development.

It first appeared in the middle of the eighteenth century, almost simultaneously in Italy (Vivaldi, Sammartini), Germany (Stamitz and the Manheim school), France (Gossec), Austria (Cannabich) and England (Johann Christian Bach). In the order of its various movements, as well as their interior structures, the symphony follows the pattern of the sonata, and it has been rightly pointed out that the symphony is a sonata for orchestra. Stylistically the symphony is distinguished by the diversity of its orchestration; the wind instruments, in particular, are far more highly individualized than in the earlier sinfonia. Haydn (erroneously called "the father of the symphony") and Mozart, drawing partly on the attainments of their predecessors, wrote the first masterpieces in this genre. In the nineteenth century the symphony acquired enormous dimensions with Beethoven, who replaced the minuet with the scherzo, expanded the orchestra and added, in one instance, a chorus. Schumann's and Brahms' symphonies were conceived on an equally large scale, and Bruckner's and Mahler's on an even larger one. The impressionists neglected the symphony, but it was somewhat revived again after World War I (*Third Sym-*

phony, by Roussel, *Symphony for Strings*, by Honegger, *Symphony in Three Movements*, by Stravinsky).

STRUCTURE.

As the symphony is constructed along the lines of the sonata, it poses no special structural problems.* Nevertheless at a time when the sonata often involved only three movements the symphony ordinarily had four: an allegro, sometimes preceded by a short introduction: a slow movement, either andante or adagio; a minuet, left over from the dance suite; and a finale, very fast. Starting with Beethoven, the minuet gave way to the scherzo, which at times was interpolated between the opening allegro and the slow movement (Ninth Symphony).

Ordinarily the internal structure of each movement follows that of the *sonata* (q.v.). However, the variety of orchestral tone color and the multiplicity of instruments require larger dimensions and more substantial developments. This is something nineteenth-century musicians may have realized a bit too well: from Beethoven on both the symphony and the symphony orchestra increased in size. In Mozart's time the orchestra consisted—aside from the string quintet sections of first and second violins, violas, cellos and bass viols—of one or two flutes, two oboes, two bassoons and two horns, to which were subsequently added trumpets and kettledrums, and then clarinets. Beethoven introduced the piccolo and the trombones, then the contra bassoon and a substantial percussion section; at the same time the string section was enlarged and the number of horns doubled

* Obviously it is impossible to here discuss or even survey the very complex aesthetic problems raised by certain key works, such as Beethoven's Fifth Symphony—problems that could be the subject of a "treatise on tonal form," involving a study of Beethoven's great attainments (the transcending of the thematic concept, the way the "raw material" governs the structure and so on).

(there are four in the Ninth Symphony). At the end of the
nineteenth century the enormous post-Wagnerian orchestra
went hand in hand with the lengthily developed symphonies
—the opponents of this music call them interminable—of
Brahms, Franck, Chausson, Saint-Saëns, d'Indy, Tchaikov-
sky, Bruckner and Mahler. It was against this bloated excess
that Schoenberg reacted, at the beginning of the twentieth
century, with his short *Chamber Symphony,* for fifteen instruments.

TIENTO

The *tiento* (*tiento,* "feeling one's way," "trial
and error") was a Spanish instrumental form, similar to the
Italian ricercare. Like the ricercare, it first appeared in the
sixteenth century, but whereas the ricercare was originally
intended for the lute, the tiento, which used the organ, dis-
played greater technical and stylistic richness. In the tientos
of Cabezón, who was the foremost composer in this genre,
we find a mixture of imitative contrapuntal writing and improvisational style, of ternary and binary rhythms, and of
diatonicism and chromaticism, all of which attest to a con-
sistently experimental approach somewhat more advanced
than that of the Italian instrumental polyphonists. The Italians caught up in the seventeenth century, as Spanish music
began to decline.

TOCCATA

Like the prelude and the fantasy, the *toccata* (from the Italian *toccare*, "to touch," "to play") is an essentially instrumental composition, but more specifically designed for performance on the keyboard: organ, harpsichord or piano. It probably came from the horn calls sounded from belfries in the Middle Ages; whence the heroic character it often assumes and the profusion of broken harmonies that its earliest forms, at any rate, display. Fairly often the toccata replaced the prelude as a prefatory piece (Toccata and Fugue in B minor, by J. S. Bach). It developed in the sixteenth century; the seventeenth was its golden age. It began to fall into disuse after the middle of the eighteenth century, reappearing intermittently in the works of a few romantics (Schumann) and moderns (Debussy, Ravel), who handle it in a rather unorthodox style.

STRUCTURE.

The toccata has no precise structure. In fact it is probably one of the least "constructed" of all instrumental forms. The oldest known compositions—notably those of Andrea Gabrieli—offer a contrast between a vertical style of writing (at the beginning of the composition) and virtuoso passages or, at times, polyphonic fragments in imitative style. In the hands of Frescobaldi and his disciples it became a meditative improvisation. J. S. Bach conceived it either as a brilliant piece full of constant contrasts (Toccata and Fugue in D minor) or as a kind of carefully constructed prelude

143

("*Dorian*" *Toccata*). The modern toccata generally employs short values; it is a virtuoso type of piece with a sustained rhythm.

TRIO

The *trio* might be succinctly defined as a three-part instrumental or vocal composition. However, the term has at least five different acceptations:

1. In the seventeenth century and at the beginning of the eighteenth, the *sonate à trois*, or trio-sonata, was often simply called a trio; paradoxically this type of composition was played on four instruments: two violins and one viola da gamba, plus a harpsichord. However, since the harpsichord's only function was to actualize the harmony implied in the bass, it was not counted as one of the real parts. Similarly at the beginning of the eighteenth century, Telemann's trio-sonatas involved only a violin and a harpsichord, the latter counting this time for two parts, which indeed it actually played. (See *Sonata*.)

2. Since the classical period the trio has become a kind of chamber sonata for piano, violin and cello (Beethoven, Schumann). However, other instrumental combinations are also possible: the most common is the *trio for strings*: violin, viola, cello (the viola is sometimes replaced by a second violin), as illustrated by Beethoven. The *woodwind trio* includes the clarinet, oboe and bassoon.

3. The *organ trio* is a three-part composition played on two manuals and the pedal board, each voice being strongly

individualized. Its writing is evidently very contrapuntal (cf. the trio-chorales and trio-sonatas in the work of J. S. Bach).

4. The *vocal trio* comes under the heading of lyric music. It has a place in opera and contata, when a situation involves three characters of equal importance (*Don Giovanni*, Act I, Scene 3).

5. *Trio* is also the name given to the central part of certain pieces with repeats or *da capo* sections, such as the *minuet* and the *scherzo* (q.v.). Here the origin of the term goes back to Lully, who sometimes scored interludes for two violins and a viola, or two oboes and a bassoon, for contrast.

VARIATION

According to the way it is considered, the *variation* is either a form, a technical device or both. Writing a variation on a theme consists in transforming it without altering its essence, whether by ornamenting it, transcending it completely or placing more emphasis on the secondary patterns accompanying it. As a form the variation embraces many others, such as the *canzone*, the *chaconne*, the *chorale* and the *passacaglia*; as a device it figures in the elaboration of almost every structure. The idea of variation is probably almost as old as music itself. Many examples of ornamental variation can be found in the Gregorian plain chant. The very principle of the mass based on the cantus firmus contains the principle of the polyphonic variation. However, the variation was not organized into a musical form until the sixteenth century; it is not known definitely whether its origin is Spanish or English. It appeared in the dance tunes played by the English violists and the Spanish lutanists of the period: many included *doubles* (divisions, or *diferencias*), which were already variations. (See *Suite*.) The diferencias written for the organ by Cabezón (middle of the sixteenth century) reveal a technique already quite highly developed, foreshadowing the Bach chorale. A little later the English virginalists carried the pre-classical variation to its highest point. The seventeenth-century masters cultivated the form in its various aspects. In the first half of the eighteenth century Handel, Rameau and especially J. S. Bach (*Chorales, Passacaglias, Goldberg Variations*) provided some famous examples of the variation. Although Haydn, Mozart and their contemporaries abandoned certain types of variation, they paid special attention to one, the *theme and variations*, which was all the rage during the first half of the nineteenth century, fostering a plethora of facile and brilliant compositions of very slight musical interest. However, the major composers, from Beethoven to Franck, continued to favor the variation. Nor has it been neglected in the twentieth century: in fact it has had a privileged place in the polyphonic revival of the Viennese school. Thus the variation, whether instrumental or vocal, seems to be the musical form that has most constantly attracted the attention of the great composers in the history of Western music.

STRUCTURE.

The principle of the variation consists in exposing the theme a given number of times in versions that may differ melodically, rhythmically or harmonically. According to Vincent d'Indy, the many methods of variation may be divided into three main categories:

1. *Rhythmic and/or melodic ornamentation.* This variation technique, without altering the substance of the theme, nevertheless modifies it intrinsically by adding supplementary notes or secondary rhythmic groups. Already used in

the Gregorian chant, this method preserves the principal stresses, the suspensive and terminal cadences and even in general the compass of the melody, its highest and lowest notes. To this type usually belong the *doubles* of the suite (Fig. 14).

2. *Polyphonic variation.* Contrary to the foregoing method, this variation technique is basically extrinsic: it does not affect the theme, which as a rule remains unchanged, but superimposes on it one or more melodic patterns, expressed in the other parts. The variation results from the combination of the different parts; this, of course, is the principle of the *passacaglia* (see this word) (Fig. 15).

3. *Thematic amplifications.* This system of variation, which is both intrinsic and extrinsic, is more subtle than the preceding ones: here the theme is not actually expressed at all; at times it is barely suggested. And yet, despite the apparent lack of reference points, the analogy between the theme and its paraphrase is often quite clear (Fig. 16).

An analogous effect results from what we might call *thematic simplification,* presumably invented by Beethoven. In thematic simplification the theme disappears almost completely; it is suggested by only one of its component elements. Thus in the fifth variation of Beethoven's Fourteenth Quartet everything related to the theme, except its harmony, is eliminated.

Schoenberg and his disciples carried the idea of variation to its furthest extreme. Starting from very sparse thematic material—normally a simple twelve-tone row—they use the variation technique to develop an entire composition on the basis of it. Although the *theme and variations* form is fairly exceptional in their work (the third movement of the *Suite,* Opus 29, by Schoenberg), the idea of continuous variation may be regarded as the foundation of their entire aesthetic system.

Fig. 14. *Les niais de Sologne* (Rameau) (rondo) and its *double*.

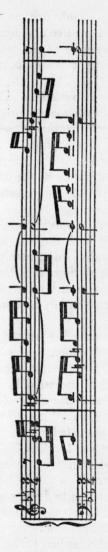

Fig. 15. *Passacaglia and Fugue* (J. S. Bach). Variation IV: the theme is in the bass.

Fig. 16. Chaconne from the Partita in D minor for solo violin (J. S. Bach).

VILLANCICO

The term *villancico* designates two very different forms, according to whether the term is applied to a composition of the sixteenth century or to a composition of the seventeenth and eighteenth centuries. The sixteenth-century villancico is a type of art song, on either a secular or a religious subject, that displays what is undoubtedly a unique combination of the popular style and the formal court style. In the seventeenth century the name *villancico* was commonly applied to a kind of cantata very close to the English *anthem* (q.v.).

STRUCTURE.

The sixteenth-century villancico comprises a series of refrains that exemplify the Spanish approach to the variation, especially in the accompanying parts, which are constantly being modified. Often there are two versions of the same villancico, one for solo voice and instruments, the other for chorus.

The villancico of the seventeenth and eighteenth centuries was identical with the church cantata as it was practiced by every European school of that period. Within this form we distinguish the *estribillo* for chorus or double chorus and *basso continuo*, and the *coplas*, or verses, reserved for the soloists.

INDEX

151